5-1 -81

CONSCIENCE IN
MEDIEVAL PHILOSOPHY

CONSCIENCE IN MEDIEVAL PHILOSOPHY

TIMOTHY C. POTTS

Lecturer in Philosophy
in the University of Leeds

CAMBRIDGE UNIVERSITY PRESS

CAMBRIDGE

LONDON   NEW YORK   NEW ROCHELLE

MELBOURNE   SYDNEY

Published by the Press Syndicate of the University of Cambridge
The Pitt Building, Trumpington Street, Cambridge CB2 1RP
32 East 57th Street, New York, NY 10022, U.S.A.
296 Beaconsfield Parade, Middle Park, Melbourne 3206, Australia

First published 1980

Set, printed and bound in Great Britain by
Fakenham Press Limited, Fakenham, Norfolk

British Library Cataloguing in Publication Data
Conscience in medieval philosophy.
1. Conscience – Addresses, essays, lectures
2. Religion – Philosophy – Addresses, essays,
lectures
I. Potts, Timothy C
171'.6'09021   BJ1471   80-40380

ISBN 0 521 23287 2

TO
JAMES AND VERA
CAMERON

Contents

Preface

I hope that this volume may help to create interest in medieval philosophy, not just as an object of purely historical study, but as an aid to thought about contemporary philosophical problems. On the face of it, medieval philosophy has been unduly neglected, accounting, as it does, for some twelve hundred years, i.e. about half, of the history of the subject. It certainly does not receive the attention which medieval history now secures from historians and there must still be many who graduate in philosophy from our universities under the impression that philosophy died with Aristotle and only came to life again when Descartes began to meditate.

The middle decades of this century were lean years for the history of philosophy in general, when it was widely thought that philosophy had made a decisive break with its past and no longer had anything worthwhile to learn from it: that medieval philosophical texts, for example, were as obsolete as medieval medical text-books such as ibn-Sina's *Canon*. In addition, there has long been a certain parochialism – nationalism, even – about European philosophy; university courses still bear witness to an emphasis upon British philosophers in Britain, French philosophers in France and German philosophers in German-speaking countries which the intellectual stature of the authors concerned does not wholly explain. The mobility of medieval philosophers and the uniformity of their cultural background makes it more difficult to claim them as products of the country in which they happened to be born.

Paradoxically, though, the greatest obstacle to widespread study of medieval philosophy has probably been the neo-Scholastic movement inaugurated by Pope Leo XIII's encyclical *Aeterni Patris* of 1879. In the first place, it led to a disproportionate concentration upon Aquinas, whose views are, on the whole, rather untypical of medieval philosophy, with the result that his work was not seen in its historical context as part of an on-going debate in the new universities of the thirteenth century, but, rather, through a Cartesian distorting-mirror. Worse still, he was enlisted in the service of Catholic apologetics and treated as an 'authority', despite the implication of his own remark 'an argument from authority which is based upon human reason is the feeblest' that there are no authorities in philosophy (*Summa theologiae* 1.1.8 *ad* 2) and his excellent advice that, when we hear a certain view expressed, we should pay no attention to *who* is propounding it, but concentrate only upon *what* is being said (*De modo studiendi*). Medieval philosophy, in consequence, became virtually restricted to clerical institutions, and philosophers elsewhere were understandably suspicious of philosopher-theologians, whether medieval or modern, whose over-riding loyalty was given to a narrowly-conceived religious orthodoxy. Ironically, the neo-Scholastic movement has been counter-productive in the long run even in those very institutions upon which it was imposed, breeding a reaction in which any pretence of studying medieval philosophy and theology has now been largely abandoned.

Nothing is more destructive of philosophy than a party spirit which approaches its history looking for a gallery of heroes and scapegoats. The latter are either ignored as unworthy of study or caricatured to provide easy targets for criticism, while the main task of philosophy is conceived to be exegesis of the former. Even that exegesis is eventually corrupted, for our heroes must have been right, so, where there is no other way to justify them, we are tempted to argue that what they really *meant* is something different from what they apparently *said*. But as Aristotle remarks somewhere, a philosopher's views are seldom entirely wrong: to which one might add, they are never entirely right, either. In any case, the point of studying the history of philosophy is not just to find the bits that are correct; we can often learn more from a philosopher who is profoundly wrong than from one who is right but superficial. This role of the history of philosophy in teaching us through the mistakes of others is, again, signalled by Aquinas. Of course, we shall no doubt form opinions as to the relative stature of past philosophers, but a good test of our objectivity will be whether we are prepared to include among the greatest some with whose doctrines we thoroughly disagree.

Rejection of the party spirit of neo-Scholasticism should not make us overlook one respect in which we are greatly in its debt. A major obstacle in the past to the study of medieval philosophy was the lack of good editions of the texts; some, indeed, were only to be found in manuscript, many others in *incunabula*, and a few in eighteenth-century editions. The neo-Scholastic movement has inspired many critical editions over the last hundred years: the Leonine edition of Aquinas is the most famous, but the various religious orders have also sponsored editions of the works of their own members, notably the Franciscans of Bonaventure and Scotus. The present volume would have been impossible without this prior textual work, for which I am not qualified. I have depended upon Lottin (1948) for his survey of medieval writing on conscience, as well as for his text of the treatise of Philip the Chancellor, upon the Quaracchi edition of Bonaventure and the Leonine edition of Aquinas. The neglect of medieval philosophy is partly explained by the absence of reliable texts; while much still remains to be edited, we do now have most of the major Latin works in an accessible form.

Translations of medieval philosophical texts into English have been heavily weighted, until very recently, towards Aquinas; nor have they been prepared with the needs of university teaching in mind. On the one hand, there are entire translations of lengthy works, on the other, anthologies which cover a large range of topics with 'snippets' from which no real acquaintance with the author's thought can be made, and which contain the work of many different translators with no coordination over such matters as the rendering of technical terms. Seventeen years' experience in teaching medieval philosophy has convinced me (after trying out various methods) that students need passages from each author long enough to obtain some idea of his style of thought and argument and that, if they are to be able to compare and contrast one author with another, passages upon the same broad subject must be taken. Conscience fulfils these requirements well, although the translations here are a small selection from the material available, which is listed more fully in Appendix 1. Among others Alexander of Hales, Henry of Ghent and Duns Scotus might have been represented.

The translations were prepared for the second-year undergraduate course in medieval philosophy in the University of Leeds, and have now been used in two sessions. I hope that they will be useful to others who are responsible for medieval-philosophy courses and, accordingly, I have included, in Appendix 2, a programme for a term's or semester's course based upon them. It is easiest to follow the texts chronologically, but less interesting and profitable than to divide them by topic and consider all of the texts upon each topic simultaneously. My programme is organised in the second way; it is more demanding of students, since they must read once through all the texts before the course begins.

It is possible to follow and understand much in philosophical texts from Descartes onwards with very little knowledge of earlier philosophy or of historical background, although misunderstanding is likely, too, and it can never be ideal to study a philosopher out of context. With medieval philosophers, however, very little understanding is possible without some background knowledge. So far as the thirteenth-century Latin philosophers are concerned, acquaintance with Aristotle is the most important pre-requisite and, as Aristotle is essentially a revisionist Platonist, that requires some knowledge of Plato's work, too. For this reason, I have included in my programme some topics from ancient philosophy, knowledge of which is presupposed in the medieval texts on conscience. Of course, it will be better still if students approaching the latter have already taken a course on ancient philosophy. Even so, however, it may be useful to revise the topics listed in the programme before going on to the medieval texts.

In addition to Aristotle, a range of Christian authors was studied in medieval universities and certain names crop up again and again in quotations, above all, Augustine, but also John of Damascus, Gregory the Great, Boethius and Peter Lombard. This common culture of western Europe in the thirteenth century differs so vastly from our own that it is often essential, in order to understand the texts properly, to make the relevant aspects of it explicit. Even medieval Christianity differs substantially, in its emphases when not in its actual doctrines, from Christianity today. All this, together with an alien literary style, places obstacles in the way of the student who wishes to relate medieval philosophical discussions to modern ones. The essay which precedes the translations is intended to remove some of these difficulties, by bringing out the relevant background and by relating the issues to contemporary ones. I hope, however, that the translations provide enough of the original texts for the reader not to be at the mercy of my interpretation of them, but to be able to form an independent judgement.

A special difficulty which attends medieval philosophy is that it is not clearly distinguished from theology. Even though some medieval authors draw a definite distinction between the two disciplines, their works commonly contain a mixture of the two and they do not differentiate, at each stage, between philosophical and theological discussion. Very often, however, it is only necessary for us to understand their theological assumptions, and not to adopt them, in order to seize the essential argument; for the theology may only reflect the common culture of the time, the view being urged in no way depending upon it. A good example in the present context is the notion of *sin*, which pervades the texts on conscience translated and discussed here. 'Sin' is a theological term, meaning 'an offence against God'. But although medieval authors nearly always speak of wrong-doing as 'sin', nine times out of ten the problems which they pose lose none of their force if the reference to God be omitted. Thus, when Bonaventure, for example, asks whether *synderesis* can be extinguished by sin, it is not essential to his problem or to his arguments that we consider specifically wrong-doing directed against God; nothing is lost if we take him to be asking whether *synderesis* can be extinguished by wrong-doing in general. Of course, a translator must render *'peccatum'* by 'sin', leaving it to the reader to make such modifications in this and comparable cases as he may deem necessary in order to extract the philosophical content of the text.

An invitation from the editors of the forthcoming *Cambridge History of Later Medieval Philosophy* to contribute a section on conscience provided the occasion for the essay which accompanies the translations in this volume. I am indebted to one of the editors, Dr A. J. P. Kenny, for criticism of an earlier version, which has led to many improvements. A shortened version will be found in the *Cambridge History*. I am grateful to my colleague Professor P. T. Geach for vetting my translations and for several corrections to them; it was he who spotted that Bonaventure's term *'dignitates'* is a literal translation of the Stoic philosophers' *'axiomata'*, thus making good sense of a passage which had previously puzzled me, and who noticed an allusion by Augustine to the four cardinal virtues, which I had not picked up. Professor W. C. Kneale directed my attention to *'synteresis'* in late Greek; until then, I had supposed that *'synderesis'* in medieval philosophy was a corruption of the Greek *'syneidesis'*. My thanks are due also to Mrs E. Harris, who has a rare ability in accurately transcribing manuscripts containing technical and, especially, Latin terminology, for preparing the typescript for the press.

Glossary

with English terms in alphabetical order

GREEK	LATIN	ENGLISH
ἐνέργεια, energeia	actus	actualisation
ἐπιθυμία, epithymia	concupiscentia (occ. cupiditas)	appetite
γνῶσις, gnosis	cognitio	apprehension
ἀξίωμα, axioma	dignitas	axiom
—	(liberum) arbitrium	choice, free
προαίρεσις, proairesis	proheresis	choice, preferential
συνείδησις, syneidesis	conscientia, synderesis	conscience
ὄρεξις, orexis	appetitus	desire
ἕξις, hexis	habitus	disposition
θυμός, thymos	ira	emotion (lit. anger)
κάθολου, katholou	universalis	general
yêtzer ha-ṭôb (Heb.)	—	impulse, good
yêtzer hâ-râ' (Heb.)	fomes (peccati)	impulse to sin
νοῦς, nous	intellectus	intellect
ἐπιστήμη, episteme	scientia	knowledge
καθ' ἕκαστον, kath hekaston	individuum	particular
αἴσθησις, aisthesis	sensatio	perception
ἡδονή, hedone	delectatio	pleasure
δύναμις, dynamis	potentia	potentiality
δύναμις, dynamis	vis	power
πρόνησις, phronesis	prudentia	practical wisdom
λόγος, logos	ratio (one sense)	reason
ἁμαρτία, hamartia	peccatum	sin
ψυχή, psyche	anima	soul
πνεῦμα, pneuma	spiritus	spirit
συντήρησις, synteresis	synderesis	synderesis
νοῦς, nous	intellectus	thought
κριτήριον, kriterion	iudicatorium	tribunal
νοῦς, nous	intellectus	understanding
βούλησις, boulesis	voluntas	will, rational desire
σοωία, sophia	sapientia	wisdom

I

Peter Lombard and Jerome

Conscience has been much neglected by philosophers. It is not directly treated in ancient philosophy, while, apart from Bishop Butler, who was primarily interested in the aspect of self-deception, there is scarcely a philosopher from Descartes to the present day who has touched upon it more than tangentially. In the thirteenth and fourteenth centuries, however, a treatise upon conscience became a standard component of commentaries upon Peter Lombard's *Judgements* and from there found its way into university seminars (written up as *Debated Questions*) and textbooks (*Summae*). The history of this development up to Henry of Ghent has been ably documented by Lottin (1948). Lottin, though, was writing for specialists in medieval philosophy and from within the tradition of the 'Gothic revival' of clerical culture, with the result that his work is not easily accessible, psychologically, to contemporary philosophers who are the intellectual heirs of Hume, Kant and, now, of Frege. My purpose is therefore to draw upon Lottin's researches in order to interpret the later medieval discussion of conscience to philosophers more closely acquainted with the subsequent development of their discipline, in the belief that the medieval contribution opened up questions which are still worth pursuing. Indeed, there has been a tendency of late towards a gap between the philosophy of mind and ethics, even to the extent that one group of philosophers has concentrated upon philosophical logic and the philosophy of mind, while a different group has concentrated upon ethics and political and social philosophy. Conscience lies within this gap: it is not obvious, off-hand, whether it is a topic in the philosophy of mind or an ethical topic, so reflection upon it may serve, apart from its intrinsic interest, to bring together again what has been sundered.

Yet the way in which conscience became a standard topic of later medieval philosophy was curious, almost an accident, while the classificatory scheme within which it was treated is so different from that of more recent philosophy as to demand a preliminary reorientation if the point of the questions which medieval authors posed is to be appreciated today. One would expect to find that the motivation for raising questions about conscience was theological and that it came into European thought from Hebrew sources; yet both the term and the topic (except at a superficial level) are Hellenistic in origin. So far as the former is concerned,

The term 'conscience' (συνείδησις) is to be understood in conjunction with a number of similar words and phrases, which are sometimes used interchangeably. These are τὸ συνειδότος, τὸ συνειδός, σύνεσις, αὐτῷ συνιστορεῖν τι, αὐτῷ συνειδέναι τι. All these stem from the verb σύνοιδα, which means 'I know in common with'. It usually implies knowledge about another person, which can be used in witness for or against him. Hence σύνοιδα came to mean 'I bear witness'. Of particular importance is the phrase αὐτῷ συνειδέναι τι, which means 'to share knowledge with oneself', 'to know with oneself', 'to be a witness for or against oneself', because συνείδησις (like τὸ συνειδός and σύνεσις) is its substantial equivalent. The necessity for finding a single substantive to convey the meaning of a phrase would be natural (Davies, 1962, p. 672).

The Latin 'conscientia' is thus an exact transliteration of 'syneidesis'. It was much more popular in ancient Latin writers than 'syneidesis' among ancient Greek authors, both Cicero and Seneca connecting it with Epicureanism (Davies, ibid.). Whether in its Greek or in its Latin form, however, the term has a range of meanings, only part of which is preserved by 'conscience' as it is now used in modern English. (I am indebted, in what follows, to Lewis 1967, though his account must be read critically and with caution.) In its weakest sense, the prefix ('syn-', 'con-' = 'with') does not modify the meaning of the noun to which it is attached, so that it is merely a synonym for 'knowledge'. It is from this sense that the modern English 'consciousness' has developed, together with the adjective 'conscious' which is often a synonym for 'aware', as in 'I'm fully conscious that . . .'. Where the prefix does modify the meaning of the noun, the original sense is that of knowing something (in company) with someone else. Since it would be rather pointless to insist upon the shared aspect of the knowledge where its object was public anyway, it was used primarily in cases where one person was privy to another's secret, and this carried two further implications. The first is that, in being privy to another's secret, I am in a position to witness to what he knows. The second (not always fulfilled) is that a man is ashamed of what he keeps secret, so that my witness, if I choose to give it, will be against him rather than to his credit.

The modern English sense of 'conscience' derives from this by two stages. Stage one is reflexivisation: being privy to one's own secret. This notion has obvious difficulties: if a man knows something, can he fail to know that he knows it? There is an everyday case which suggests that he can. Sometimes a person, when asked a certain question, replies 'I don't know', but then, after further questioning, comes out with the answer, so that we say to him: 'You see, you really knew all the time.' He had temporarily forgotten the answer, but not to the extent of being totally unable to recall it: he just needed some prompting. This is part of what is involved in examining one's conscience: you go over the events of a previous period in order to call to mind what you did or failed to do, and often remember thereby a number of things which you had temporarily forgotten. The exercise is necessary because, if they are things of which we are ashamed, it is highly convenient to forget them.

On closer scrutiny, though, this turns out to be more than a mere reflexivisation of being privy to *another's* secret. A case of the latter could be described by a sentence obtained from the schema:

(S1) A knows that B knows that p

where 'know' bears the same sense in *both* occurrences. It could be purely dispositional, even to the extent that B had temporarily forgotten that p and that A had temporarily forgotten that B knew that p. We can imagine circumstances in which we said to A: 'You see, you really knew all the time that B knew that p'. This is not possible in the reflexive case, which can be described by sentences derived from the schema:

(S2) A knows that he himself knows that p.

If A has temporarily forgotten that p, then (S2) will be false. So the first occurrence of 'know' must mean 'is aware that', though, of course, A need not actually be thinking of what he knows about for it to be true (cf. Hintikka 1962, pp. 103–125). The reflexivisation of (S1) to yield (S2) thus involves a restriction of the meaning of the first occurrence of 'know', such that (S2) has the same truth-conditions as 'A is aware that he knows that p' or 'A is conscious that he knows that p'. Otherwise, the consequence holds that

(C1) A knows that $p \vDash A$ knows that he knows that p

and, since the converse is merely a special case of

(C2) A knows that $p \vDash p$

(with 'A knows that p' substituted for 'p'), (S2) is equivalent to 'A knows that p'. Thus the weak sense of '*conscientia*' must be imported in order to drive a wedge between merely knowing that p, and knowing that one knows that p.

A person who has successfully examined his conscience is then in a position to *witness* as to what he did or failed to do; customarily, however, he will also *judge* his actions or omissions as right or wrong in the circumstances, by measuring them against his standards of behaviour. If they meet these standards, we say that he has a 'good conscience', if not, that he has a 'bad conscience' (and then he normally feels guilty). Logically, there is a transition from being witness to being judge but, psychologically, recall and judgement are often simultaneous. Because of this, the second stage in the development of the meaning of 'conscience' has been its application to a person's standards of behaviour, and this is now the central sense in modern English. In order to understand the medieval discussion of conscience, this development must be borne in mind. In particular, we need to ask whether the final stage has broken the original connection between conscience and knowledge: people's standards of behaviour differ, so are they not a matter of belief rather than of knowledge? As a first attempt at explaining what we mean by 'conscience' today, we might well say that it is the set of beliefs held by a person, say A, which can be reported in the form:

S3) A believes that he ought to ϕ,

where any verb of action, or corresponding verb-phrase (which may include a sign of negation), may be substituted for 'ϕ'. Borrowing from the branch of modal logic which treats of what is obligatory, forbidden or permitted, I shall call a belief which can be reported in this form a *deontic* belief. If, however, the connection of conscience with knowledge is to be sustained, the relevant schema will be

(S4) A knows that he ought to ϕ,

and this entails, where (S3) does not, 'A ought to ϕ'. In this case, I shall speak of 'deontic knowledge'.

Even in speaking of deontic belief, I am assuming that sentences obtained from the schema 'A ought to ϕ' can be either true or false. This has been challenged by some philosophers, but is taken for granted by medieval authors. *Prima facie*, the assumption appears to be well-founded: to believe something is to believe that it is *true*, so schema (S3) would be semantically ill-formed if no sentence obtainable from the schema 'A ought to ϕ' had a truth-value. Yet it is a matter of everyday experience that people *do* hold beliefs about what they ought to do, and it is difficult to see how any investigation of conscience would be possible if this were not so. In particular, how could we raise the question, of interest alike to medieval and to contemporary philosophers, whether a man is always obliged to follow his conscience? – for this is equivalent to asking whether there is a valid consequence from schema (S3) or from schema (S4), according to the account of conscience which one adopts, to 'A ought to ϕ'.

But this is to anticipate, for the majority of medieval discussions of conscience are to be found in commentaries on Peter Lombard's *Judgements* 2.39, where the question is not directly about conscience at all but, rather, how the will can be bad. As usual, Peter Lombard reports several answers, though, exceptionally, he does not pronounce judgement upon them at the end. He notes, first (1.3) that some people distinguish two senses of 'will' (*voluntas*), in one of which it is a power, in the other the exercise of that power. This, of course, is Aristotle's distinction between potentiality and actualisation, but a new application of it. If the will is represented in propositions whose main verb is 'want', i.e. in those obtainable from the schema

(S5) A wants to ϕ,

then it would appear always to be dispositional: such a proposition can be true even when A is fully engaged in activities which have nothing to do with the desire which it reports. Moreover, the most natural way of construing 'exercise of the will' would be as describing any action intended to secure the fulfilment of the desire in question, where such action would not normally itself consist in willing or wanting. This seems to have been Aristotle's own view, since he says that the conclusion of a piece of practical reasoning is an action (*De motu animalium* 6, 70ᵃ111–20).

The distinction which Peter Lombard reports, however, was more probably inspired by a passage in which Aristotle distinguishes between two senses of 'know', the first dispositional, but the second actually thinking about what one knows, as is sometimes necessary when using one's knowledge (*De anima* 3.4, 429ᵃ29 ff.). Similarly, we each have a host of desires, but it is only at certain times that any one of them makes itself felt or that we pay attention to it, so that it is then actualised in the sense of being called to mind. The problem which Peter Lombard sets out requires this interpretation, for, he continues, the will is part of man's natural endowment, and he rejects the solution that *qua* potentiality it is always good but *qua* actualisation sometimes bad, on the ground that there is nothing wrong with calling to mind what one knows, so why should there be anything wrong with calling to mind what one wants? He admits, though, that there may be some occasions when it may be bad to call to mind what we know: 'For now and again a person remembers something bad in order to do it, and seeks to understand the truth in order to attack it' (2.1).

Yet these are exceptional, rather than typical cases, whereas evil desires are commonplace, and this leads him on to the famous passage in Romans 7 where St Paul describes his own internal conflicts: 'For I do not do what I want, but do what I do not want' (v. 15). Are there, then, asks Peter Lombard, two wills in man? Those who say 'Yes' fall into two camps. The first group holds that the will by which a man wants to do what is good in such a conflict is the will with which he is naturally endowed; it is the spark of conscience which, as Jerome said, was not even extinguished in Cain, whereas the other will is a result of the Fall of Adam. The second group takes the opposite view: the will by which a man wants to do what is bad is embraced by free choice and is in the ascendant unless and until God's grace gives greater strength to the will that wants to do what is good. Finally, there are those who maintain that there is only one will in man, by which he 'naturally wants what is good and through a defect in it wants and takes pleasure in what is evil; so that, to the extent that it wants what is good, it is naturally good but, to the extent that it wants what is bad, it is evil' (3.4). Peter Lombard concludes by remarking that the question whether there are two wills in man is a deep one, leaving it to his successors to decide between the three solutions.

Conscience is thus no more than mentioned by Peter Lombard, and then only with the reference to Jerome in his report of the first opinion. It arises, moreover, in the context of a conflict of desires. Subsequent writers followed up the reference to Jerome, which is to the beginning of his *Commentary on Ezekiel* (see Translations, pp. 79–80). It makes a much more explicit connection between conscience and Plato's (rather than St Paul's) discussion of conflicting desires, and consists of an allegorical interpretation of the four animals in Ezekiel's vision (Ezekiel 1:4–14), which gave Jerome's medieval readers many headaches. They were not worried by his exegesis: the text of Ezekiel and its meaning plays no further part in the discussion. In his vision, Ezekiel saw four living creatures coming out of a fiery cloud. Each of them had the form of a man, but with four faces; the front face was human, the right face that of a lion, the left that of an ox, and the back face that of an eagle. Jerome interprets the four faces as representing the structure of the human soul, correlating the first three faces with Plato's tripartite division in the *Republic* (4, 436B–441B). Peter Lombard's citation of Jerome is thus very apposite, for Plato invokes the tripartite division precisely to explain a conflict of desires. We must now go into this in more detail, as it is closely relevant to the medieval discussion.

Plato's argument proceeds in three stages. First, he establishes with the aid of an example that 'the same thing will never do or undergo opposites in the same respect in relation to the same thing and at the same time; so if we meet these contradictions, we shall know that it was not the same thing, but a plurality'. Thus, if a man who is standing still moves his hands and head, we cannot properly say that he is simultaneously at rest and in motion, but only that a part of him is at rest and a part in motion. Second, he applies this principle to desire and aversion: people who are thirsty are sometimes nevertheless unwilling to drink (as a modern example, take the alcoholic to whom apomorphine has been administered; he has a desire for a drink but, simultaneously, an aversion to it, because he knows that it will have an extremely unpleasant effect – vomiting, etc.). In this example, both the desire and the aversion have the same object, so Plato concludes that they must have different subjects. There is no room for distinguishing different parts of the alcoholic's body for this purpose and, hence, we must posit different parts of his soul. His aversion to the liquor is rational, so its subject must be the rational part of the soul, whereas his desire for it is non-rational, a kind of appetite; its subject can therefore be assigned as the appetitive part.

In the final stage of his argument, Plato introduces the story of Leontios to show that a third part of the soul must also be admitted:

Leontios . . ., on his way up from Piraeus under the outer side of the northern wall, becoming aware of dead bodies that lay at the place of execution, simultaneously felt a desire to see them and a repugnance and aversion, and . . . for a time he resisted and veiled his head, but overpowered in despite of all by his desire, rushed up to the corpses, opening his eyes wide and yelling at them: 'There you are, curse you! Take your fill of the splendid sight.'

Leontios is angry with himself for yielding to his desire; but isn't this anger just a manifestation of his rational aversion to the deed? 'No', replies Plato, because small children, in whom reason has not yet developed, throw tantrums when their appetites are frustrated, so anger (and, more generally, the emotions) can sometimes side with reason, sometimes with appetite. Hence we must posit an emotive part of the soul in addition to the rational and appetitive.

The doctrine of the tripartite soul was not inherited by the middle ages in its pure form, but in the modified version adopted by Aristotle. Aristotle had considerable hesitation, in the *De anima*, about speaking of 'parts' of the soul; he discusses this terminology several times, rather inconclusively, but prefers on the whole to apply his potentiality/ actualisation distinction here instead and to regard the soul as having rational, appetitive and emotional potentialities rather than parts. They are nevertheless conceived as basic and mutually irreducible psychological potentialities and thus preserve the Platonic idea of the human soul as having a structure. Little then hangs upon the use of 'part': a structure consists of inter-related parts, but the parts can be of any logical type, so Aristotle is merely taking Plato's analysis one step further and specifying parts of the soul as potentialities.

It is common today for the tripartite soul to be rejected by philosophers, but Plato's argument is more difficult to evade than may at first sight appear, and it has exerted a very far-reaching influence upon European thought. Moreover, it is this framework which presented medieval philosophers with their central problem about conscience, for Jerome's suggestion is that the soul has a quadripartite structure, with conscience as a fourth potentiality irreducible to any of the other three. Yet one possible interpretation of the Leontios story is that he had a bad conscience about looking at the corpses, his subsequent anger with himself being a manifestation of guilt. More generally, chronic conflicts of desires are typically cases of wanting to do something but believing (or, perhaps, knowing) that one ought not to do it. So is not conscience an aspect of reason, rather than a distinct potentiality? Yet, on the other hand, it also seems to involve the emotions: a person who acts against his conscience normally feels guilty.

These are the initial problems which medieval philosophers saw in Peter Lombard and Jerome, but they are not the first questions about conscience which a modern philosopher would ask. Still, I think that the medieval approach can be justified. Plato, it may be objected, failed to notice that 'want' may be followed by a second verb, and that, even in sentences in which a second verb does not appear, one can be understood as implicitly present. In his own examples, the second verb is explicit: thus the correct description of the man who has conflicting desires about drinking is that he both wants to drink and wants not to drink. Nor is this description overtly contradictory: the 'not' qualifies 'to drink'; it does not qualify 'want'. Certainly the man cannot fulfil both desires simultaneously, but he can have them without thereby forcing us to admit a different subject for each desire. But anyone who takes this view must also deny that

(C3) A wants not to $\phi \vDash A$ does not want to ϕ

is a valid consequence, since, otherwise, we can immediately obtain a contradiction from the original description. And if this case is the only reason he can give for denying its validity, then his resort will be suspect. It would be an even feebler solution to say that the sense of 'want' in which the man wants to drink is different from that in which he wants not to drink, for, if that were so, why should he feel any internal conflict between the two desires? The second stage of Plato's argument thus survives the necessary correction that in 'A wants not to ϕ', 'want' does not fall within the scope of 'not'.

We find no problem in regarding the human body as having a structure. Moreover, we cannot ascribe to human beings *qua* bodies the full range of qualities which we *do* ascribe to them. A man may kick a ball with his foot or lift a glass to his lips with his hand, but with what part of his body is he mean or witty, stupid or lazy? We regard human beings as persons, too, and it would surely be surprising if human personality, which we understand so much worse than human bodies, did not also have a structure. Psychiatrists and psychologists, at any rate, find the assumption necessary. Perhaps the former here have been influenced by ancient and medieval ways of thought; we know, for example, that Freud attended a course of lectures on Aristotle in Vienna, and the elements of his 'tripartite soul' are evidently related to three of Jerome's four: the 'I' to reason, the 'It' to appetite and the 'Super–I' to conscience. But the same charge cannot be brought against a psychologist like Cattell, who has used factor analysis in order to isolate and identify basic personality traits which, upon inspection, appear very close to potentialities. The medieval preoccupation with psychological topology is thus not, after all, so alien to modern thought, and we do not have to commit ourselves to a particular classification of basic potentialities in order to profit from their discussions: indeed, within limits, they differ among themselves about the best classification.

Jerome also raises the question whether a person can cease to have a conscience. This is still topical (cf. Ryle, 1958) but, today, it would probably be discussed in conjunction with the related question whether a person can fail to acquire a conscience. The latter is a blind spot of medieval philosophers; they lacked our notion of psychopathic personality and it did not occur to them that conscience might be environmentally determined by parents, education and society. This is perhaps the greatest weakness of the medieval discussion, but it is understandable in a society which did not manifest the variety of deontic belief commonly encountered today and in which there was little communication with and knowledge of other cultural traditions. In spite of this, their answers to Jerome's question led them eventually to issues which lie at the heart of the topic. For Jerome's own answer is, *prima facie*, inconsistent.

First, he tells us that even Cain did not cease to have a conscience, a rather surprising remark in view of the story of Cain and Abel, for at no point in the story does Cain show the slightest sign of being sorry for having murdered his brother. When the Lord asks him, 'Where is Abel your brother?', he tries to disown any responsibility: 'I do not know; am I my brother's keeper?' (Genesis 4:9). Subsequently, after being sentenced to a nomadic life, he merely complains: 'My punishment is greater than I can bear' (Genesis 4:13). However, Jerome then goes on to say that very wicked people *do* cease to have any conscience, quoting other passages of Scripture in support.

Medieval philosophers thought they could resolve this inconsistency. Jerome introduces the example of Cain in apposition to '*synteresin*', 'that spark of conscience which was not even extinguished in the breast of Cain . . . and by which we discern that we sin'. Now '*synteresin*' could be a corruption of '*syneidesis*', but there is also a late (and rather rare) Greek word '*συντήρησις*', of which it is an exact Latin transliteration. This is a compound of '*τηρέω*', which means 'watch over', 'heed' or 'observe'. '*Synteresis*' most commonly means 'preservation' or 'maintenance', as e.g. in God's conservation of his creation. But the '*syn-*' prefix can also have reflexive force, which gives it the sense of observing or watching over oneself and, perhaps, thereby preserving oneself from wrongdoing. Jerome's quotation from 1 Corinthians suggests that this is how he understood it, for the verb which St Paul used in that passage was '*tereo*' ('keep sound' in the translation). Yet Jerome goes on to say that 'this conscience is cast down among some people . . . and loses its place'. This suggested to medieval philosophers that a distinction should be drawn between synderesis (Greek '*ντ*' is pronounced 'nd') and conscience, synderesis being the 'spark of conscience' rather than conscience proper. Thus, they note that, even when a person does not feel guilty about having done something which is wrong, he may still regret the consequences, e.g. a punishment inflicted upon him on that account, and to that extent regret having done it.

This residue of regret is then regarded as the 'spark of conscience', which can plausibly be attributed even to Cain, since he complains about his punishment.

There thus grew up two treatises, one on *synderesis* and the other on *conscientia*, the two notions being so expounded that *synderesis* cannot be lost but *conscientia* can. To medieval philosophers, this would have seemed an honest attempt to make sense of a puzzling passage in Jerome, although, as exegesis, it will hardly convince a modern reader. For when Jerome says that *this* conscience *loses its place* in some people, he must be referring to its place in the quadripartite structure of the soul, where the fourth part is said to be *synteresis*. It is, admittedly, curious that he used '*synteresis*' in preference to '*syneidesis*', since he would have known that the latter was the exact equivalent of the Latin '*conscientia*'. But he is reporting the views of others (of which no independent record survives), so he would have felt obliged to use their terminology, while indicating by his remark about conscience losing its place that he supposed them to mean 'conscience' by '*synteresis*'. His comment upon Cain would then have to be construed: '*synteresis*, i.e. conscience, of which some spark was left even in the breast of Cain . . .'. He may well, indeed, have been attributing Cain's remorse on account of the consequences of his action to a residue of conscience, but it is also debatable whether this attribution is correct. A man might, for example, be unjustly punished for something which he did, and regret having done it because of the consequences, even though he neither feels guilty about what he has done nor has any reason to do so. In this case, his regret has nothing whatever to do with conscience.

Disagreement with the medieval interpretation of Jerome does not necessarily force us, though, to write off the distinction between *synderesis* and conscience as an unfortunate mistake. There could be independent reasons for drawing a distinction *within* what we simply call 'conscience' – never mind the labels for it – and the right question to ask is whether the medieval distinction, in spite of its muddled origin, turned out to be productive. Do the two terms mark a distinction which is essential for understanding and speaking clearly about the notion of conscience? If so, then the original motivation for its introduction need not trouble us further.

2

Philip the Chancellor

The first treatise on conscience, which set the pattern for subsequent ones, was written by Philip the Chancellor about 1235. Philip deals primarily with *synderesis* and only secondarily with *conscientia*. He poses four questions; *conscientia* does not make its appearance until the third, in which it is distinguished from *synderesis*. A modern reader is not likely to make much of the first two questions – whether *synderesis* is a potentiality or a disposition, and how it is related to reason – until he has some grasp of Philip's distinction between *synderesis* and *conscientia*, so we need to go straight to his discussion of the third question.

It is set out in the usual scholastic form: arguments that *synderesis* can lead us to do wrong, arguments that it cannot, discussion and, finally, replies to or comments upon the initial arguments. The first argument to show that *synderesis* can sometimes lead us astray begins: 'Conscientia is sometimes mistaken, sometimes right. But in whatever power there is any mistake over what is to be done, in that power there is sin' (Translations, p. 102). Well, then, Philip continues, citing Jerome, *synderesis* is the same as *conscientia*; so *synderesis* can lead us to do wrong. In his discussion, however, Philip denies that *synderesis* is the same as *conscientia*; the latter, he says, comes from a conjunction of *synderesis* with free choice. He then gives an example to illustrate this:

suppose that it is written in *synderesis* that everyone who makes himself out to be the son of God and is not, should die the death; but that this man (pointing to Christ) makes himself out to be the son of God, yet is not: it is then supposed: therefore he should die the death. What was contributed by *synderesis* was unchangeable and dictated only good, but this conjoined with what was contributed by reason dictated sin. So, therefore, *synderesis* plus the reason for a free choice makes *conscientia* right or mistaken, and *conscientia* sticks more to the side of reason; *synderesis* itself, however, which is the spark of *conscientia*, ... is not mistaken (Translations, p. 104).

A closely related example occurs in the fourth question. There, the first argument to the effect that *synderesis* can be lost is that the *conscientia* of many heretics dictated to them that they should undergo martyrdom in order to defend their faith, but that this was a sinful mistake. Thus *synderesis* did not murmur in them in answer to sin (Translations, p. 105). Philip's reply is as follows:

the effect of *synderesis*, considered as such, is paralysed in them because of the lack of faith, which is the basis of everything good. But the exercise of *conscientia* thrives in them, the evidence of which is that the man is ready to undergo martyrdom, because he supposes what he believes to be the faith. It is not, however, *synderesis* which does this, but what belongs to free choice or reason. Moreover, *synderesis* is not extinguished in such a person because, although he may be mistaken about the particular matter, evil in general still displeases him . . . This is shown by the conversion of many, upon recognising their mistake . . . And it is like someone who knows in general that every she-mule is sterile, and yet believes that this she-mule is pregnant; when he studies and thinks it over, the mistake goes away . . . (Translations, p. 107).

These two passages should be taken in conjunction with an addendum to the second question, where the distinction between general and particular again comes to the fore:

synderesis affects free choice by telling it to do good and restraining it from evil, and moves us to the general good which is found in this or that good deed. Hence it is not in itself directed to particular good deeds, but to the general [good] which is present in them. Moreover, there is no deliberative judgement in *synderesis*, only executive. For it determines the good in any particular good deed without deliberation (Translations, pp. 101–102).

Philip's argument is thus that we need to distinguish between *general* and *particular* deontic propositions because, in spite of holding a correct general principle, a person can always misapply it to particular circumstances and so mistakenly believe himself obliged to a certain action. If both are subsumed under the single, undifferentiated notion of conscience, then, faced with examples of the type which Philip cites, we cannot answer the question: 'Is the man's conscience mistaken?' If, however, we distinguish between *synderesis* and *conscientia*, then we can say that his *synderesis* is not mistaken but his *conscientia* is. But we then need a more precise characterisation of the difference between a general and a particular deontic proposition and, apart from his examples, Philip does not give us this. In particular, his examples do not settle conclusively whether 'general' ('*universalis*') should be interpreted narrowly, to include only universally quantified propositions, or, more widely, to include existentially quantified ones as well.

Quite apart from this, Philip's account still leaves us with a problem, though, because even the modern distinction between general and particular propositions is not exclusive. If a proposition contains a verb which, in the simplest case, would still have to be combined with more than one proper name or deictic expression in order to yield a sentence, then it can always be combined partly with proper names or deictic expressions and partly with quantifying expressions. In addition, it can also be combined with definite descriptions, and philosophers are presently much divided as to whether these should be classified with proper names or with quantifying expressions. So the question arises: how general must a general deontic proposition be in order to qualify as a possible object of *synderesis*? Must it be wholly devoid of proper names and, perhaps, of definite descriptions as well?

There is one case which is likely to occur immediately to a modern reader in this connection which must be dismissed as irrelevant to the medieval discussion. Since Kant, it has commonly been held that the dictates of *synderesis* must be 'universalisable'. Thus, to illustrate the point from one of Philip's examples, if a man merely believed that he himself ought to be prepared to die for his beliefs, but that the corresponding obligation did not necessarily bind others, that could not count as a dictate of *synderesis*. He must also believe (or know) that *everyone* ought to be prepared to die for his beliefs. This is a requirement that a universally quantified expression should occur in the subject-position of a deontic proposition for it to be a proper object of *synderesis* (the expression may, of course, be qualified by a relative clause importing a condition, i.e. be of the form 'everyone who . . . ought to . . .'). Medieval writers do not discuss this aspect of the generality of deontic propositions. They are concerned, rather, with the type of expression substituted for 'ϕ' in schema (S3) or (S4).

The expression substituted for 'ϕ' may be just a verb, as in 'Philip believes (knows) that he ought not to steal.' Stealing, though, is an action which involves three parties: not only has someone to do the stealing, but there has to be something which he steals and someone from whom he steals it. The example thus implicitly contains quantifying expressions and, normally, these would be construed as universal; thus it can be spelled out as meaning that Philip believes that he ought not to steal anything from anyone. There is even a further implicit universal quantification over time: he believes that he ought *never* to steal anything from anyone. Perhaps we are applying deontic propositions of this type in the majority of cases where our conscience impels us to do some particular action, but certainly not in all. Philip, for example, no doubt believed that every Christian ought to obey the laws of the

Church. There is *some* generality here, in that 'the laws' means 'any laws', but also some particularity, in that the Church is a particular society. Again, a Muslim believes that he ought to visit Mina at least once in his lifetime. In both of these cases, it is not immediately obvious that the respective deontic beliefs are themselves applications of some yet more general one. Are they, then, too particular in content to be possible contents of *synderesis*?

Philip's *motivation* for distinguishing between *synderesis* and *conscientia* is that he wants to maintain that, although *conscientia* can be mistaken *synderesis* cannot. His *ground* for distinguishing between them, however, is that general propositions can be misapplied to particular circumstances. We must be careful not to confuse the ground with the motivation. He gives us a good reason for drawing a distinction between two senses of 'conscience' but, in accepting this, we are not compelled to agree that, in one of the senses, conscience cannot be mistaken. This remains as a further question; it was, indeed, controversial even at the time, for he was taking issue with William of Auxerre (cf. Lottin, 1948, p. 150). Philip's examples certainly do not settle it, because we could just as well, in support of a distinction between *synderesis* and *conscientia*, have cited cases in which the general proposition was false but was misapplied to yield a particular one which was true. Philip's motivation restricted his choice of examples. Jehovah's Witnesses, for instance, believe that one ought not to have a blood transfusion. Suppose, then, that a Jehovah's Witness refuses permission for his child to receive a blood transfusion, although he has been told that, without it, the child will die. In fact, however, the physician is mistaken; unknown to him, the child has a rare condition in which a blood transfusion will be fatal and, in any case, the child will recover without it. By acting in accordance with his conscience the Jehovah's Witness thus saves his child's life. His *synderesis* is apparently mistaken but, through ignorance of the facts, he applies it to circumstances to which it is not germane, with the result that his *conscientia* is correct. In order to ring changes with examples, I have here imagined a case in which the misapplication of the general proposition is due to ignorance of fact, but we could easily modify Philip's she-mule example to yield a corresponding misapplication due to invalid reasoning. Again, we cannot answer the question: 'Was his conscience mistaken?' without distinguishing between *synderesis* and *conscientia*, yet examples of this type argue that *synderesis* can be mistaken just as much as *conscientia*.

If we accept that *synderesis* can be mistaken, though, we must say that it consists of the set of our general deontic *beliefs*, not of our general deontic *knowledge*, for beliefs can be false, whereas knowledge cannot. Medieval writers accounted *synderesis* as a form of knowledge, and they can claim a good deal of support from common ways of speaking about conscience. We speak of *knowing* the difference between right and wrong; on particular occasions, we may tell someone: 'You *know* you ought to do such-and-such' or 'You ought to have *known* better than to do that.' This does not imply that we can never be mistaken about the truth-values of general deontic propositions, but only that there are at least some cases of deontic knowledge and not just of deontic belief, *synderesis* being reserved for them. A person can *think* that he knows something when, in fact, it is false; in that case, he does not know it, and it is not part of his knowledge: it is just a false belief. We should then merely have a special case of this when someone thinks he knows that he ought to ϕ (with some general expression substituted for 'ϕ') when it is false that he ought to ϕ.

If there is any deontic knowledge, we might wish to mark the distinction between deontic knowledge and deontic belief by reserving '*synderesis*' for a person's deontic knowledge. But let us be clear that this draws the line between *synderesis* and *conscientia* differently from Philip's distinction between general and particular deontic propositions. The former are no more immune to falsity than the latter, while, *per contra*, if a person knows that he ougnₜ to ϕ (a general proposition) and correctly applies this to particular circumstances, then he will also know that he ought to perform some specific action. Moreover, it will not even be enough to guarantee that it is part of his *synderesis* that a deontic proposition which he holds is both true and general, for this might just be a case of true belief and not of knowledge. Philip's distinction between general and particular deontic propositions, accordingly, will not simultaneously mark out a distinction between *synderesis* and *conscientia* and yield the result that *synderesis* cannot be mistaken.

Philip also holds that *conscientia* involves free choice, whereas *synderesis* is non-deliberative. The same motivation is at work here: only where choice comes into play is wrong-doing possible. To a modern reader, it may not be evident, however, that his examples involve choice in their misapplications of general deontic propositions. In the first, a man points to Christ and says: 'That man claims to be the son of God, but is not'; the judgement of *conscientia* then follows as the conclusion of a deductive argument from the premiss that people who falsely claim to be the son of God should be liquidated. In the second, a man holds certain heterodox religious beliefs but, of course, thinks that they express the true faith; again, the judgement of *conscientia* is a deductive conclusion from the premiss that a Christian should be prepared to die rather than abjure his faith. From Philip's point of view, though, acceptance of the minor premiss in each example involves free choice. In the first, he is thinking of the Jews who rejected the claim of Jesus to be the son of God and prosecuted him for blasphemy, and he is adopting the viewpoint of the gospels from which their rejection is seen as wilful. Similarly, heresy, in medieval eyes, was equally a wilful rejection of religious truths and the heretic could never be in good faith.

Although we may not agree with Philip's interpretation of his examples, there is no need to argue about it. It is unnecessary, even, to challenge the underlying assumption that belief is not just an intellectual matter but commonly involves an element of choice (cf. Potts, 1971). For, even if that be granted, the role of choice in belief can be greater or less, so that we have a spectrum of cases with, at one extreme, choice playing no part at all. Typically, it will play a greater part in religious, political and deontic beliefs, but little or no part in many of our more trivial beliefs. So we can easily concoct examples which, like Philip's, support a distinction between *synderesis* and *conscientia* but which afford no ground to posit choice as a factor in assent to the minor premiss. Suppose that a man believes that he ought to give alms to the poor, but mistakenly believes of a certain very rich widow that she is destitute. He may simply have been misinformed about her; it could be a purely factual mistake, without any motivation in his desires. So he concludes that he ought to give alms to this widow. Here, too, we cannot straightforwardly answer the question: 'Is his conscience right or wrong?' Using Philip's distinction between *synderesis* and *conscientia*, though, we can say that his *synderesis* is right but his *conscientia* wrong. One could even imagine a case in which assent to a general deontic proposition was motivated by an evil desire, but was combined with a purely factual mistake about some circumstances to yield a correct particular deontic conclusion. A man might persuade himself, for example, that a certain type of action was in general wrong, producing a rationalisation so that he did not have to admit to himself that it would be extremely convenient to his own interests and advantage if it were forbidden, yet might quite rightly judge that the action would be wrong for him to do in some special circumstances, though it was wrong not for his reasons, but for others of which he was ignorant.

It seems, then, that Philip is again asking his distinction between general and particular deontic propositions to do too much work and that he has been misled by his choice of examples. In this case, though, recent philosophy has opened up a line of defence which, though not available to Philip, can be used to defend him. So far, I have been very careful to stick exactly to Philip's own characterisation of the *synderesis*/*conscientia* distinction in terms of that between general and particular deontic propositions. But his examples also invite another interpretation: we might say that *synderesis* consists of *rules*, whereas *conscientia* is concerned with their application (including misapplication). Of course, this re-interpretation immediately raises the question whether general deontic propositions are co-extensive with rules of the relevant type. It is certainly not clear that generality is a mark of rules in general; one has only to think of the rules which are given for the use of some piece of machinery in the instruction booklet which comes with it, e.g. 'the red wire should be attached to the plug terminal marked "L"'. Very little consideration, indeed, has yet been given to the logical form of rules, so perhaps the most that can be said at present is that replacing the distinction between general and particular deontic propositions with that between a rule and its application *may* amount to a substantial modification of the *synderesis*/*conscientia* distinction as conceived by Philip.

Still, if we are prepared to entertain this interpretation, it provides the necessary leeway for choice in *conscientia*. For a rule can never dictate its own application. However detailed it may be, a *decision* is always required as to whether it applies to a given situation. The latter must be brought under the description contained in the rule, and this depends upon seeing the situation in a certain perspective, for any situation can be variously described from different points of view. It may sometimes be more natural to adopt one view-point rather than another, but nothing forces us to do so. Yet do we always *choose* our view of the situation? Well, at least our desires can often prompt us to describe an action in one way rather than another: a man whose *synderesis* tells him that he ought not to steal, and who has appropriated a book belonging to someone else, may find it extremely convenient to describe himself as merely borrowing the book, on an extended loan, so that the rule against stealing will not apply. Granted, he may not have been conscious of making a choice in settling upon that description of his action, may not have considered and rejected the alternative, but we do not restrict choice to selection between alternatives: 'Well, you chose to do it' can be said to someone whenever he *had* an alternative, even if he did not consider it.

The time for choice may also lie in the past. A man may have got into the habit of looking at situations from a certain perspective, so that, when a new case arises, his response to it is automatic. By now, he has no choice about how to describe it, because his approach has been set long ago and just one description strikes him as natural and obvious. This case would not, I think, have worried a medieval philosopher, who would have said that, such a cast of mind having been voluntarily acquired in the past, a man is not absolved of responsibility for its later consequences because he can no longer change it, or do so only with great difficulty. Choice is involved, even if only indirectly. We, however, should be much less confident that all such habits of mind are voluntarily acquired, and hold that the ways of describing situations which seem natural to us are, to a large extent, absorbed involuntarily from our environment – family, school, society – in the course of our upbringing. In that case, it becomes important to distinguish the *logical* gap between a rule and its application, which can never be closed, from the *psychological* gap, which can be closed by *training* people to look at situations so that they describe them in one way rather than another. Indeed, if *synderesis* consists of a set of rules for guiding behaviour, they are more likely to have been acquired by generalisation from training in particular situations than by having been learned directly. A child is not likely to have been told, in the first instance 'You must not steal' and subsequently to have learned when the rule applies; he is much more likely to have been told 'You mustn't take that toy, because it belongs to Billy' and only much later, if at all, be told the rule 'It is wrong to steal'. But for medieval philosophers, as I remarked earlier, the idea of conscience being formed by training was a blind spot; if we except this, then the psychological possibilities for choice in how to describe a given situation will coincide with the logical possibilities. This could even be argued for the case of the rich widow cited earlier; if the man thinks she is destitute because someone told him so, then he has ultimately chosen to believe his informer (even if he now has a credulous cast of mind), because he could always have checked what he was told before assenting to it.

Three distinct issues thus arise out of Philip's third question. First, do we need to distinguish two senses of 'conscience'? Philip's answer to this is affirmative, and I have argued that he is right. But there are difficulties about the basis of his distinction, which rests upon differentiating general from particular deontic propositions. Moreover, his examples, together with others which support the need for some distinction, admit of an alternative basis, the difference between a rule and its application. Second, Philip contends that *synderesis* cannot be mistaken. His distinction between *synderesis* and *conscientia* does not justify this view but, if there is any deontic knowledge, then we may need a second distinction, between a person's deontic knowledge, on the one hand, and his deontic beliefs (which need not necessarily all be false), on the other. Third, he holds that free choice is involved in *conscientia* but not in *synderesis*; again, he does not justify this, but it could be defended if we take the rule-and-application interpretation of the distinction and set aside training as a factor in determining the way we describe various situations. If training is not set aside, then the furthest we can go with Philip is to agree that free choice is *often* involved in *conscientia* (on either interpretation), but not always.

We may now turn to Philip's first and second questions. His concern in asking these is to understand how *synderesis* fits into the structure of the soul. In his answer to the second, he tries to clarify the relationship between *synderesis* and reason, while the first is a classificatory question, asking whether *synderesis* is a potentiality or a disposition. Philosophical and theological considerations are closely intertwined in his treatment of these questions, which presupposes a wide-ranging background knowledge of his readers. The distinction between a potentiality and a disposition derives, with modification, from Aristotle; the main theological doctrine which impinges upon the classification of *synderesis* is that of original sin.

Aristotle conceived of a disposition as a half-way house between a potentiality and its actualisation. This model was suggested, above all, by skills, where the transition from native ability to action involves two stages: first one has to learn how to perform the kind of activity in question and then, knowing how, one is in a position to do it when occasion arises. We say of a person who knows how to do something that he *can* do it, and he will still be *able* to do it even when he is not actually doing so. So, if a thing's potentialities comprise what it can do and what it can undergo (its active and passive potentialities), a skill is a potentiality. On the other hand, it is also natural to think of a person who sets out to acquire a skill as developing his potentialities, the latter now no longer being skills but the native endowment in virtue of which he is *able to learn* the skill. These potentialities have to be exercised in order to acquire the skill and so, from this point of view, the skill is an actualisation of them; in Aristotelian terminology, their 'first actualisation'. In addition to skills, virtues and vices, even knowledge and beliefs were assimilated to this model as dispositions.

Yet, in spite of the term 'first actualisation', Aristotle tends to regard dispositions more as potentialities than as actualisations. He distinguishes rational from irrational potentialities by the criterion that the former can have contrary actualisations, whereas the latter cannot, citing a knowledge of medicine as an example, on the ground that it can be used both to heal people who are ill and to make healthy people unwell (*Metaphysics* 9.2). Here, then, a skill is given as an example of a potentiality. Elsewhere, however, a disposition is regarded as already embodying a tendency to one of two contrary types of action, making that one easier to perform and the corresponding contrary more difficult, e.g. a virtue or a vice.

One reason for this indeterminacy of classification may be that 'disposition' has two senses. In the first, it is closely connected with being disposed to do something. Thus we speak of someone as having a cheerful disposition, a quiet disposition or a moody disposition, meaning that he has a tendency or inclination to behave in a certain way. In the second sense, a disposition is an ability to do or undergo something which, perhaps, one is not actually doing or undergoing. An ability does not necessarily carry the corresponding tendency: a man who can speak Greek *may* have a tendency to come out with Greek expressions at the slightest excuse, but he might equally be very diffident about speaking Greek and do so only when no other means of communication was available to him. The connection between the two senses is that both a tendency and an ability dis–pose a man to do something, i.e. put him in a position whence it is easy to do. In the first case, however, it will be difficult for him to abstain from doing it whereas, in the second, he will usually be able to choose quite freely whether or not to exercise his ability.

An ambiguity about contrariety encourages the assimilation of the two types of disposition. To take Aristotle's example, knowledge of medicine, restoring to health people who are ill is a contrary exercise of the skill to making healthy people ill, in the sense that the two processes are converses. But we should also think of the latter as a *misuse* of medical knowledge, in that making healthy people ill is a *bad* use of the skill, and 'good' and 'bad' are also contraries, but not converses. Probably any ability can be misused but, to complicate matters, it may not be neutral as between good and bad applications. If we wanted to train medics who were efficient at making healthy people ill, we should need to modify the medical syllabus fairly substantially because, even though some parts would remain the same, much of the present syllabus presupposes that the aim of exercising the skill will be to cure people who are ill. An ability may therefore embody a direction towards a good or bad exercise of it. But even if it does, this is quite independent of whether its exercise brings about a change whose converse would also be brought about by exercising the same ability. For instance, the construction of a building demands a variety of skills, and the same combination of skills could be exercised in order to demolish a building; yet there is nothing intrinsically good about construction nor intrinsically bad about demolition: either could be good or bad according to the circumstances. There are also many skills whose exercise does not have a converse: driving a car, for example. That does not prevent them from being misused, though. Whether or not a skill is being misused, however, depends upon the *intention with which* it is exercised, i.e. whether the state of affairs which will terminate the change effected by exercising the skill is a good or a bad one in the circumstances. Moreover, this is so notwithstanding that most skills embody a direction towards good: we learn them because, in general, the fruits of their exercise are beneficial to ourselves and to others.

Tendencies, by contrast with skills, are very largely related to incompatible types of behaviour and, because of this, themselves pair off with contrary tendencies. Galen's description of the four types of human character is a classical example: the melancholic is the contrary of the sanguine, the choleric of the phlegmatic. Or, in more recent studies of personality, we find an opposition between the extrovert and the introvert. In these cases, the extremes are usually regarded as bad, a tendency in either direction to be avoided. In some respects, this is the model to which Aristotle assimilated virtues and vices, each virtue requiring a man to hold his balance between a pair of contrary vices. Here there is an interplay of two contrarieties, which do not coincide: the virtue is the good disposition, while both of the vices corresponding to it are bad dispositions, but the two vices are contrary dispositions in relation to the type of behaviour used to define them, while the behaviour associated with the virtue is intermediate.

A question which would immediately occur to a medieval philosopher trying to classify *synderesis* would thus be whether it has a contrary, and we find an affirmative answer in the second argument cited by Philip to show that it is a disposition:

> Since the soul is not abandoned by its creator so that it has no help in doing what is good, just as it contains an impulse to sin inclining free choice towards sin or evil, so, therefore, there will be some aid which, to the extent that it works of itself, always directs it towards what is good and makes it shun what is bad, in the same way as the impulse to sin is related to it contrariwise. But what else can this be except *synderesis*? Therefore *synderesis* will be an aid outside the substance of the soul just as the impulse [to sin] is not of the substance of the soul (Translations, pp. 96–97).

This argument contains a presupposition which must be expounded before discussing the 'impulse to sin' which is posited as the contrary of *synderesis*. The presupposition is that anything which is 'outside the substance of the soul' is a disposition rather than a potentiality. It leads us, directly, into the theological background to the discussion, the doctrine of original sin.

In order to sharpen the distinction between potentialities and dispositions, medieval writers customarily restrict the former, in their psychological application, to potentialities for acquiring dispositions, while the latter, following Aristotle (*Nicomachean Ethics* 3.5,1114^{b}26 ff), are regarded as *voluntarily* acquired: a man is responsible for his dispositions. The potentialities or powers of the soul are thus part of a man's native endowment. But there is an important difference between the medieval notion of native endowment and ours: *we* think of people as varying in the hereditary component of their personalities, and in two ways. First, in having different character traits (though it may often be a matter of dispute to what extent they are hereditary or environmental in origin). These would not count as potentialities of the soul in the medieval sense, which restricted them to what all men have in common (privations, like blindness, apart) in virtue of being human. Second, even with potentialities of this kind, such as intelligence, we think of people as differing from one another in *degree*; e.g. one man can learn such-and-such a skill, another cannot, because the first is *more* intelligent than the second. Although ancient and medieval philosophers sometimes advert to these differences, they play no part in the discussions with which we are concerned here. In both respects, then, potentialities of the soul are always aspects of what it is to be human. The effect of these restrictions, however, is to leave unclassified a wide range of psychological qualities which are neither potentialities of the soul nor voluntarily acquired dispositions.

Moreover, in understanding psychological potentialities as what is 'within the substance of the soul', medieval writers also exclude anything which is an effect of original sin. Anything which is proper to *fallen* human nature is 'outside the substance of the soul', so, in deciding whether a given quality is a potentiality of the soul, they considered both the state of Adam before the Fall and the human nature of Christ (who was exempt from original sin) to be relevant. This plays an explicit part in the argument quoted above, because Philip regards the 'impulse to sin' as an effect of the Fall, one of the 'wounds of human nature' consequent upon original sin. I have used the phrase 'impulse to sin' to translate '*fomes peccati*', but this is a very peculiar piece of Latin, for the normal meaning of '*fomes*' is 'tinder' or 'fuel', which makes no sense in this context; in late classical Latin it can sometimes mean 'incitement', which is at least a psychological notion, but still does not fit the context at all easily, for incitement requires someone or something to do the inciting. So what is this *fomes peccati*?

I have not been able to trace the steps by which the term entered medieval theology but, if we remember that the context of this discussion of conscience is Peter Lombard's question, 'Does a man naturally want what is good and freely serve sin by the same will, or not?', and that he relates it to the chronic conflict of desires described by St Paul in Romans 7: 13–25, it is extremely probable that the argument cited by Philip reflects the rabbinic doctrine of the two impulses in man, the evil impulse, *yêtzer hâ-râ'*, and the good impulse, *yêtzer ha-ṭôb*. According to the rabbis,

the nature of the evil impulse is to urge or incline man to all sorts of sins. It seems, moreover, that it was especially, though not exclusively, connected with sexual sins, sexual passion or lust; it was the force that led men particularly to unchastity and idolatry. Nevertheless, although some passages present God as repenting that he had made the evil inclination, the latter is also regarded as being somehow good; it is not evil in itself, . . . but only in so far as man is impelled by it to evil acts. It is the urge to self-preservation and propagation in a man and can therefore be put to good use . . . the chief means of protection against the evil impulse was study of the Torah . . . at the age of thirteen it was generally recognized that a boy is made a 'son of commandment' – *bar mitzwâh*, i.e. he becomes morally responsible and is received into the community. There were discussions also as to when the *yêtzer hâ-râ'* entered a man . . . Most of the Rabbis held that it was at birth . . . the *yêtzer hâ-râ'* was thought to be thirteen years older than the *yêtzer ha-ṭôb* in the life of every man; for that period it reigned alone when man was not morally responsible. It was at the age of thirteen that the struggle of the Two Impulses began. It was, then, with the coming of the Law that the *bar mitzwâh* would become aware of the exceeding sinfulness of sin . . . Moreover, from what we have said about the largely sexual nature of the *yêtzer hâ-râ'*, it would be the commandment ... which would generally worry any sensitive *bar mitzwâh* (Davies, 1970, pp. 21–25, summarising Strack–Billerbeck, 1928, and Moore, 1927).

The rabbis held that the struggle between the two impulses is unceasing from the age of thirteen onwards. It is, thus, a chronic conflict of desires of exactly the type which St Paul describes and, as a pupil of the rabbi Gamaliel, he would certainly have been familiar with the doctrine. However, he uses a different phrase, 'the law of sin', instead of a direct Greek translation of '*yêtzer hâ-râ'*', perhaps because he wants to make the contrast with the Mosaic law more explicit. In both cases, however, it is the individual's internalisation of the two 'laws' which gives rise to the conflict. This, too, is thoroughly rabbinic:

> The opportunity or the invitation to sin may come from without, but it is the response of the evil impulse in man to it that converts it into a temptation. It pictures in imagination the pleasures of sin, conceives the plan, seduces the will, incites to the act. It is thus primarily as the subjective origin of temptation or more correctly as the tempter within, that the *yêtzer hâ-râ'* is represented in Jewish literature. Since it compasses man's undoing by leading him into sin, it is thought of as maliciously seeking his ruin, a kind of malevolent second personality (Moore, 1927, I, pp. 481–482).

St Paul's remedy for the conflict is, necessarily, quite different from the rabbinic solution; study of the Mosaic law, with accompanying internalisation, is, on his view, only going to intensify the conflict. But here we touch upon the central contention between Christianity and Judaism; for present purposes, it is fortunately not necessary to pursue it. The more important Pauline modification in the present context is that subjection to the 'law of sin' is a consequence of the Fall, and hence is not attributable to God's design for human nature.

The rabbinic doctrine of the two impulses lends itself very neatly to superimposition upon the Platonic analysis of conflicting desires. With its emphasis upon sexual appetite, the rabbinic description of the evil impulse aligns very naturally with Plato's notion of appetite, for, although many kinds of sexual desire which would, for the rabbis, have been disordered, would not have been so for Plato, and, although the appetite described in the story of Leontios is more a morbid curiosity than a bodily appetite, Plato is in general distrustful of bodily appetites and exalts the life of reason as the path to enlightenment. Whether St Paul follows the rabbis in regarding the law of sin as working primarily through bodily appetites is more controversial, though his opposition of the spirit to the flesh readily lends itself to this interpretation.

However, we are not concerned here with Pauline exegesis in its own right but, rather, with the perspective in which medieval writers would see his treatment of chronic conflicts of desires. In forming that perspective, St Augustine played a major role.

The story of St Augustine's conversion, as he related it in his *Confessions*, is probably the most famous in the whole of literature after that of St Paul on the road to Damascus, and would certainly have been familiar to any medieval writer. Augustine's conversion was preceded by a period during which he experienced a chronic conflict of desires. This conflict centred precisely upon his sexual desires and he described it almost as a commentary on the passage in Romans 7 (*Confessions*, book 8). Moreover, his own experience seems to have influenced his view of original sin, for he expounded 'the law of sin which dwells in my members' (Romans 7:23) as consisting in bodily appetites (*concupiscentia*, cf. *De nuptiis et concupiscentia* 1.23) and especially in sexual appetite (*libido*, cf. *De gratia Christi et de peccato originali* 2.34). We are not to imagine, he tells us, that in Paradise the genitals would have been aroused by the heat of sexual appetite (*ibid.* 35) and the reason why, after the Fall, Adam and Eve were ashamed of their nudity was precisely because they discovered themselves now subject to sexual appetite (*ibid.* 36). This appetite is now present in all sexual activity, but when the latter is engaged in for the purpose of reproduction within the context of marriage, 'in as much as marriage is good, it also effects much good from the evil of sexual appetite, because it is reason and not sexual appetite which makes good use of sexual appetite' (*ibid.* 34). Even so, however, the parents generate 'sons of the flesh' and so transmit to them only what is generated; the regeneration effected by baptism cannot be inherited (*ibid.* 40). Christ alone was born without sin, precisely because he was conceived by the Virgin without bodily appetite playing any part (*De nuptiis et concupiscentia* 1.24).

St Anselm subsequently made an important modification to Augustine's doctrine, arguing that original sin does not itself *consist* in bodily appetites, but in a disorder of the will of which bodily appetites are an *effect* (*Liber de conceptu virginali et originali peccato* 3–4). This paved the way for a distinction, already found in Philip's treatise, between bodily appetites and the impulse to sin. It appears that the rabbis did not clearly distinguish the two, because they conceived the impulse to evil as having been part of God's original design for human nature, while Augustine went to the other extreme in regarding bodily appetites themselves as a result of the Fall. Two Aristotelian doctrines must have been influential in bringing people to see the necessity for a distinction here. First, Aristotle's notion of soul answered the question: 'What makes the difference between organisms and other bodies?' *not* the question 'What makes the difference between human beings and other animals?' So, plants, animals and men all being organisms, soul was to be ascribed to each. Moreover, the potentialities of any organism at one level are included among the potentialities of any organism at the next higher level: animals, like plants, can absorb nourishment and grow: men, like other animals, have perception and bodily appetites. But only men have reason. Second, Aristotle distinguished between the theoretical and the practical aspects of the soul. The theoretical side is concerned with apprehension of the environment and, hence, aims at truth; the practical side with changing the environment and, hence, at what seems good to the organism in question. At the level of reason, the distinction is illustrated by reasoning which is directed to discovering the truth, contrasted with reasoning which is directed to action. At the next level down, apprehension of the world is effected by perception, whereas animals are moved to change it by their bodily appetites. So the structure for the human soul which emerges is a 2 × 2 matrix. In the present context, we are only directly concerned with the practical 'column', in which the two 'rows' are occupied, respectively, by rational desire and bodily appetites. But what corresponds to the latter in the theoretical column is perception and, since no one had ever thought of saying that perception is not part of God's original design for human nature, it would be incompatible with this model to suggest that bodily appetites were a result of the Fall. The model can be retained, however, if we distinguish between bodily appetites, potentialities of the soul which are, in themselves, good, and the *disordered* bodily appetites of those in whom they are not fully subject to the control of rational desire. The impulse to sin is, then, the tendency of bodily appetites to over-ride reason which is a result of the Fall.

Hence if *synderesis* is the counterpart of the impulse to sin, it should be related to rational desire as the impulse to sin is related to bodily appetites. This does not necessarily mean that *synderesis*, too, will be a result of the Fall, only that it will be a tendency of practical reason (rational desire) which 'boosts' the latter in the opposite direction to that in which the impulse to sin 'boosts' bodily appetites. There are, indeed, three possibilities each of which would be compatible with regarding *synderesis* as the counterpart to the impulse to sin. First, it could be an acquired tendency developed in order to counteract the impulse to sin, comparable in certain respects to virtues; this is the rabbinic solution, in which the *yêtzer ha-ṭôb* is developed through study of the Law (an exercise of reason). Second, it could be a special gift of God to help men to cope with the effects of the Fall; this is one of the solutions reported by Peter Lombard:

Others, however, say that there is a mental motivation by which the mind, having abandoned the law of higher things, subjects itself to sins and is attracted by them. Before grace is present to someone, this motivation, according to them, tyrannises and rules over man and suppresses the other motivation . . . When grace comes, the bad motivation is crushed and the other, naturally good one is freed and helped so that it is effective in wanting what is good (Translations, p. 93, 3.3.).

The third possibility is that *synderesis*, although not a potentiality, is an innate tendency of rational desire: in terms of the doctrine of original sin, what remains after the Fall of the full control of bodily appetites which obtained before it. This is Philip's solution. His motivation for rejecting the other two possibilities, though not explicit, can be inferred. The first would not have fitted into his scheme of classification, which did not provide for acquired dispositions which are not voluntarily acquired, while the second would have carried the awkward consequence that those persons exempt from original sin – Adam and Eve before the Fall, Christ and, according to some medieval writers, the Virgin Mary – would have had no *synderesis*, because they had no impulse to sin which needed a counter-balance.

Philip develops his solution in answer to his second question, how *synderesis* is related to reason. His strategy is to distinguish four senses of 'reason'. We can ignore the first and second, which are very hospitable, and go straight to the third, which is the use, by now familiar, in contrast to appetite and emotion. *Synderesis*, he maintains, is part of reason in this sense, what remained of

the original righteousness of man's powers, which Adam had in the state of innocence, which remained as a little light leading him to God, lest he should be turned or bent to temporal things by his entire reason . . . For it is established that Adam was naturally righteous by virtue of his judgement, will and emotions . . . And each of these looks to the highest good, to which it primarily relates. It will not, accordingly, be a potentiality separated from these powers to the extent that they are pliable, but will exist in them inflexibly, the same as each one of them (Translations, p. 100).

By 'pliable', he means that they can be directed towards good or bad, whereas *synderesis* is inflexible, being always directed towards good. Philip thus rejects Jerome's suggestion that conscience is a distinct potentiality; indeed, he expounds Jerome as saying no more than that conscience is above the three Platonic powers in worth, because it cannot be deflected from good. For all that, Philip does not make his position clear in this passage. Its Anselmian content is evident; yet, at the end, he says that *synderesis* exists *in* reason (and emotions), then, immediately after, that it is 'the *same* as each one of them'.

He attempts a further precision by considering the question in relation to a fourth sense of 'reason', in which reason is contrasted with understanding as well as with appetite and emotion. This distinction between reason and understanding derives from Augustine, although Augustine uses the terms 'knowledge' and 'wisdom' respectively (*On the Trinity* 12). He argued, in Platonic vein, that reason can be directed either to what is subject to change or to what is unchangeable. The first is necessary for the conduct of our everyday lives, but involves imagination in that it feeds upon perception; it results in knowledge and is directed towards action. The second consists primarily in thinking about God but also, more generally, about any eternal truths; it results in wisdom and is directed towards contemplation. Augustine thus distinguished wisdom from knowledge roughly as Plato distinguished knowledge from belief.

As it stands, this is no more than a distinction between possible *objects* of thought. It is not, yet, a distinction of potentialities and, indeed, understanding is frequently referred to as 'higher reason', while reason as contrasted with understanding is called 'lower reason'. This *could* be construed merely as a way of differentiating two aspects or uses of a single potentiality, much as the Aristotelian distinction between theoretical and practical reason, though it could also be taken as dividing the Platonic potentiality into two. But the interest of this passage in Philip's treatise does not lie in any contribution to the difficult question of how potentialities are to be distinguished. The point to be seized upon, rather, is that he places *synderesis* in understanding, for this contains an implication that goes beyond his requirement that its contents will be described by means of *general* deontic propositions.

If *synderesis* lies in understanding, then its contents must be *unchangeable*. Hence, the corresponding deontic propositions will be *necessary* and, if misunderstanding is excluded, necessarily true. General propositions, by contrast, even those which are universally quantified throughout, may be contingent, e.g. 'No one over fifty becomes an astronaut'. Universality and necessity were widely assimilated in ancient and medieval philosophy (cf. Hintikka, 1957), so Philip probably did not realise that he was propounding two distinct constraints upon *synderesis*. But it is important for *us* to notice the difference because, in the subsequent medieval discussion, the requirement of necessity assumes an increasing role.

Philip's account of the relationship of *synderesis* to reason still does not settle, though, the issue whether it is a potentiality or a disposition. In spite of the confusing passage noted above, however, a measure of clarification has emerged. First, he holds that it is innate and not acquired. Second, that it is not a grace to compensate for the impulse to sin, but what remains of the full control of bodily appetites which man possessed in the state of innocence. Third, that it is not a potentiality distinct from reason in the Platonic sense. Fourth, that it relates to higher rather than to lower reason. It can hardly, though, be identified with higher reason, for the latter is concerned with theoretical as well as with practical matters, and the general (or perhaps necessary) deontic propositions with which *synderesis* is concerned serve as premisses of practical reasoning. Yet Philip is not prepared to classify it as a disposition:

Synderesis, although the morphology of its name makes it sound more like a disposition than a potentiality, is nevertheless the name of a dispositional potentiality: I do not say of an acquired disposition, but of an innate one. And thus, *qua* disposition it can be applied to what is related to it as a disposition, *qua* potentiality to what is related to it as a potentiality. From this it follows that it has a certain opposition to . . . the impulse [to sin] and sensuality . . . *qua* potentiality, it is disparate from . . . sensuality . . . So, if anyone asks whether it is a potentiality or a disposition, the right answer lies in taking something in between: a dispositional potentiality (Translations, p. 97).

The reference to the etymology of *synderesis* is, of course, that it is a compound of *oida* and that knowledge is a disposition.

The term 'dispositional potentiality' was Philip's own invention; in part, the idea, already to be found in William of Auxerre, is that a dispositional potentiality is one more easy to actualise than one of the 'basic' psychological potentialities (cf. Lottin, 1948, p. 139n.). A cynical view of Philip's solution is that he is just trying to have the best of both worlds and to avoid having to contradict openly the authorities whom he cites on each side. This would not do him justice. The details of his treatment which have been expounded and discussed in this section show that he faced a familiar problem in philosophy: he had inherited a system of classification which was too simple to cater for the complexity of the phenomena which he was trying to describe. There is a close modern parallel: Wittgenstein found, when he tried to classify psychological concepts, that the traditional categories were inadequate (cf. especially 1967, §§ 472 ff). Thus, if we ask whether pain is a sensation or an emotion, the right answer is that it has certain features in common with sensations but others in common with emotions. Wittgenstein, indeed, resisted the temptation to invent a new category, say of emotional sensations, into which pain could be fitted; but we must remember that modern methods of classification are much more sophisticated than medieval ones, and one way of taking Philip's solution is not to place great weight on his category of dispositional potentialities, seeking to define it more exactly, but, rather, to construe his major contention as being that *synderesis* is in some ways akin to a potentiality and in others to a disposition. It is like a potentiality, according to him, in being innate, but like a disposition in embodying a tendency, namely, to what is good.

Philip's treatise opened up a series of important questions relating to conscience, but it did not provide definitive solutions to them. Medieval philosophy, indeed, never reached a consensus upon the topic. Instead, two main positions crystallised out of the subsequent discussion; I have taken Bonaventure as representative of the first and Aquinas as representative of the second. Aquinas followed Philip's lead more closely than Bonaventure's but Bonaventure pursued two major features of Philip's treatment, bringing them together: the idea that *synderesis* is innate, and the idea that its objects are unchangeable.

3

Bonaventure

By the time of Bonaventure, it had become customary to divide treatises upon conscience into two parts, one devoted to *synderesis* and the other to *conscientia*. But Bonaventure and other Franciscan writers take *conscientia* first. In addition, Bonaventure does not draw the distinction between *synderesis* and *conscientia* in the same way as Philip. The first question in each section of his treatise has practically the same form: 'Does *conscientia* belong to the thinking or to the desiring part of the soul?' 'Is *synderesis* to be classified with apprehension or with desire?' Bonaventure's questions are thus apparently posed in relation to the Aristotelian distinction between the theoretical and the practical aspects of the soul but, when we delve into the details, Bonaventure's taxonomy turns out to be more complicated.

It will be best to approach this matter obliquely. First, Bonaventure does not appeal to any distinction between general and particular deontic propositions in order to differentiate *synderesis* from *conscientia*, though he does report Philip's view, without committing himself to it (2.1). Instead, he immediately quotes John of Damascus with approval to the effect that conscience is the law of our thought, since, says Bonaventure, 'a law is what we recognise by means of *conscientia*' (1.1). But this, for Bonaventure, does not distinguish *conscientia* from *synderesis*, for he tells us later (2.1) that both of them are related to natural law. However, he continues, natural law can be understood in two ways: first, as a set of injunctions, second, as a psychological disposition. As a set of injunctions, it is the object of *conscientia* and *synderesis*, the latter telling us them and the former inclining us to observe them; but, whereas *conscientia* is a disposition of practical reason, *synderesis* is a desiring potentiality because it tends towards what is good. *Synderesis*, he adds, is related to *conscientia* as charity is related to faith.

It will already be clear that Bonaventure's conception of the difference between *synderesis* and *conscientia* is quite different from Philip's. He is distinguishing two aspects of conscience which are combined in Philip's notion of *synderesis*, namely, that it involves both reason and desire. The set of deontic propositions which Bonaventure terms 'natural law' has to be *known* but, once known to a person, he will in some sense *want* to act in accordance with them. Bonaventure's position also involves an implicit rejection of the 2 × 2 matrix classification of the structure of the soul which was described in the last section. He accepts, indeed, a distinction between theoretical and practical and also one between apprehension and desire but, for him, they do not coincide. Thus, in his discussion of the question whether *conscientia* pertains to thought or to desire, after distinguishing three senses of *conscientia*: its object (that of which we are conscious, i.e. the natural law), the potentiality of being conscious (ability to become conscious of the natural law) and the disposition in virtue of which we are conscious of the natural law (knowing it but not continuously exercising our knowledge), and observing that the last sense is the most usual one, he continues:

If, then, it be asked of what potentiality it is a disposition, it should be said that it is a disposition of the potentiality of apprehension, but in a different way from theoretical knowledge, because theoretical knowledge perfects our thought to the extent that the latter is theoretical, whereas *conscientia* is a disposition perfecting our thought to the extent that it is practical, or to the extent that it directs us towards deeds. And thus thought has a motivational aspect, not because it effects change but because it tells us to do something and turns us towards doing it. Such a disposition is, accordingly, not just called 'knowledge' (*scientia*), but '*conscientia*' so as to signify that this disposition does not in itself perfect the theoretical potentiality, but does so as joined in some way to desire and deed. Because of this, we do not say that conscience dictates premises like 'every whole is greater than any of its parts', but rightly say that it tells us 'God is to be honoured' and similar premises, which are like rules for what is to be done (Translations, p. 111).

Conscientia, for Bonaventure, is thus both apprehensory and practical. In saying this, he is trying to do justice to two features of schema (S4): first, that it reports a piece of *knowledge*; second, that the deontic proposition which it contains is a premiss of *practical* reasoning. But this, in his view, still does not explain the sense in which a person who knows that he ought to φ thereby also *wants* to φ, so, he argues

just as the intellectual part [of the soul] has, since its very creation, a light which is a natural tribunal for it, directing the intellect towards what can be apprehended, so too desire has a certain natural bias, directing it to what is desirable. There are two kinds of thing which are desirable: some are honourable, others useful, just as there are two kinds of thing which can be apprehended, some being theoretical, some to do with behaviour. And just as '*conscientia*' only names judgement which is directed to behaviour, so '*synderesis*' only names that bias of the will, or the will with that bias, which makes it turn to good things which are honourable (Translations, p. 116).

The analogy which Bonaventure draws, between theoretical versus practical apprehension and desire for what is honourable versus desire for what is useful, introduces a new cross-classification which elaborates the 'rational' row of the earlier one. The columns are now 'apprehension' and 'desire' respectively, while rational apprehension is divided into theoretical and practical, rational desire into desire for what is honourable and desire for what is useful.

The analogy which Bonaventure sees will probably not be so clear to us. The honourable and the useful might be understood as an attempt to apply to desire Augustine's distinction between higher and lower reason, construing what is honourable as what is good for its own sake and what is merely useful as what is good for the sake of something else, i.e. as a means to some further end. Desire for what is honourable would then be akin to contemplation in having no further *raison d'être*, but desire for what is useful be aimed, rather, at the concerns of everyday life and securing its necessities. There is, indeed, some evidence that Bonaventure has the Augustinian distinction in mind in these passages. But theoretical versus practical apprehension does not correspond with higher versus lower reason; theoretical apprehension includes knowledge of contingent facts, while practical apprehension, it would seem, includes knowledge of non-contingent deontic propositions.

Bonaventure is surely right in stressing that conscience involves both apprehension and desire, even should it be a species of belief rather than of knowledge. It is also, certainly, practical in that it relates to action and to good and bad. So he is justified in his dissatisfaction with a classification of potentialities which assimilates the distinction between apprehension and desire to that between the theoretical and the practical. But if conscience involves two distinct potentialities, one by which deontic propositions are apprehended, the other by which we have a corresponding desire to abide by them, then it should be possible to imagine beings who had the first potentiality but not the second, so that they knew (or believed) that they ought to do such-and-such, yet had no desire to do it, evinced not by their failure to do it, but by a total absence of any remorse for their failure. Yet is it not part of the *meaning* of schema (S4) and even of (S3) that such a corresponding desire is simultaneously present, i.e. that (S5) follows as a valid consequence? If so, then beings who had the first potentiality but not the second could not have *our* concept of obligation, or, to put the situation more exactly, could not have the first potentiality either, if that is a potentiality to apprehend deontic propositions in which 'ought' has the same meaning as it has in our language.

Although Bonaventure does not advert to the question of meaning in this connection, he does so in another, which provided him with an opportunity to make an important contribution to the debate about conscience. His second question about *conscientia* is whether it is an innate or an acquired disposition, and his answer is that it is partly innate and partly acquired. Arguing against Philip, he quotes Aristotle to the effect that even our knowledge of basic premisses (whether of theoretical or of practical reasoning) is acquired from memory, perception and experience. He then fastens upon a passage at the end of Augustine's discussion of the distinction between higher and lower reason, in which Augustine gives his own interpretation of the dialogue between Socrates and the slave-boy in Plato's *Meno* (*On the Trinity* 12.15). Augustine rejects the Platonic interpretation that the slave-boy is recollecting something that he had known before birth. But instead of making the now familiar point that a diagram can serve as a proof in mathematics, and that the questions which Socrates puts to the slave-boy direct his attention to certain features of the diagram which Socrates has drawn, Augustine suggests that the slave-boy saw the answers by means of a mental illumination which is the analogue of light in vision.

Bonaventure extends this suggestion to deontic knowledge:

since it is necessary to apprehension that two things should be present concurrently, namely what can be apprehended and light by means of which we judge the former, as we see in the case of sight and as Augustine suggests . . ., apprehensory dispositions are partly innate because of a light imparted to the soul, but also partly acquired because of forms . . . For everyone agrees that there is an imparted light of the apprehensory potentiality, which is called a natural tribunal, but we acquire forms and likenesses of things by means of the senses, as Aristotle says explicitly in many places and as experience also teaches us. For no one would ever apprehend *whole* or *part*, or *father* or *mother*, unless he received its form through one of the external senses; . . . However, that light or natural tribunal directs the soul itself in judging both of what can be apprehended and of what can be done . . .

Since '*conscientia*' thus names a disposition which directs our judgement with respect to what can be done, it follows that in one way it names an innate disposition with regard to basic dictates of nature, but an acquired disposition with regard to what is added by education. It also betokens an innate disposition with respect to a directing light, but an acquired disposition with respect to the form of what is itself apprehensible. For I have a natural light which is enough to apprehend that one's parents are to be honoured and that one's neighbours are not to be harmed, but I do not have the form of *father* or form of *neighbour* naturally impressed upon me (Translations, pp. 113–114).

Translating Bonaventure's talk of forms into modern terminology, his contention in this passage is that all knowledge is acquired to the extent that no one can formulate a thought until he has a stock of concepts, since thoughts are composed by combining concepts in various ways. But once having formulated thoughts, there are some whose truth is known to us by the 'natural light' of reason alone, without recourse to further experience. These are the basic premisses both of theoretical and of practical reasoning, an example of the former being the thought that any whole is greater than each of its parts and of the latter that a man should honour his father and his mother. The 'natural light' of reason is thus, roughly, what we should call 'insight', a moment of illumination in which we *see* that a certain thought, whether theoretical or practical, is true. Bonaventure's analogy with light and vision is not forced; it permeates a great deal of our vocabulary concerned with learning, knowledge and understanding. The learner suddenly *sees* the point of something: it *dawns* on him (perhaps in a *flash*) and becomes *clear* at last; these are just a few examples, which could easily be multiplied.

Bonaventure does not, however, hold that *all* deontic propositions are known innately:

the following point is especially to be noted. Just as certain things which can be apprehended are exceedingly plain, e.g. axioms and primary premisses, but some things are less plain, e.g. particular conclusions; so, too, some things which can be done are maximally plain, e.g. 'Do not do to others what you do not want to be done to you', that one ought to submit to God, and so on. Apprehension of basic premisses is therefore said to be innate to us in virtue of that light, because that light is enough to apprehend them by, once the forms have been assimilated, without any further persuasion, on account of their own clarity. Thus apprehension of the basic premisses of behaviour is innate to us, in that the ability to judge is enough to apprehend them by. Moreover, apprehension of the particular conclusions of [the various branches of] knowledge is acquired in that the light which is innate to us is not enough to apprehend them, but demands some persuasion and a new aptitude. This is also to be understood as applying to deeds, which are things to be done and to which we are bound, which we only apprehend by additional education (Translations, pp. 113–114).

Bonaventure is drawing a comparison between practical and theoretical reasoning in this passage and is relying on Aristotle's model of an academic discipline (earlier version in the *Posterior Analytics*, later version in *Metaphysics* 4: cf. Potts, 1976, for a fuller discussion) for his picture of theoretical reasoning. The 'basic premisses' are those which are common to all disciplines, e.g. tautologies. They are, according to

Aristotle, combined with premisses proper to a particular discipline to yield conclusions, which in turn are taken as the premisses of further arguments. Thus the development of the discipline consists in constructing chains of deductive argument.

Although the only discipline for which this model is plausible is mathematics, Bonaventure's comparison yields a valuable point which, although he himself assimilates it to Philip's distinction between general and particular deontic propositions, is new. This is to the effect that the basic premisses of practical reasoning may be combined with other premisses, not necessarily deontic, to yield deontic conclusions, which are nevertheless not *applications* of the rules expressed by the basic premisses to the particular circumstances of an individual, but rules with a more specific content than the basic premisses from which they are derived. His example is that the Jews, arguing from the basic deontic premiss that God is to be obeyed, conclude that circumcision and the dietary prescriptions of the Mosaic law are still obligatory (2.3 *ad* 4, Translations, p. 120). The suppressed non-deontic premiss is that God commands male children to be circumcised and the observance of certain dietary practices; from Bonaventure's point of view, as a Christian, these commands have now been withdrawn, so the premiss is false. *Conscientia* is thus infallible only in its apprehension of basic deontic premisses, for which reasoning is not required.

Curiously, Bonaventure rejects the view that the apprehension of basic deontic propositions is an exercise of higher reason. If they are known to us by a 'natural light', once we have acquired the requisite concepts, without recourse to further experience, they would appear to be clear examples of the unchangeable truths which, according to Augustine, are the objects of higher reason. Bonaventure's ground for rejecting this conclusion is that the exercise of higher reason always involves reasoning; as he puts it, 'the higher part of reason, however, does not name that potentiality of the soul in which it is moved *naturally*, but in which it is moved *deliberatively* (2.3 *ad* 2, Translations, p. 120). Thus, he continues, there can be sin in higher reason, e.g. loss of faith and despair, which are directly opposed to theological virtues. *A fortiori*, the apprehension of basic deontic propositions cannot be an exercise of lower reason, so it is puzzling where Bonaventure can fit it in.

Bonaventure's view of *conscientia* is thus a prime example of the ethical doctrine which has since become known as intuitionism. It is, however, a relatively sophisticated version of that doctrine, for he does not suppose that we simply 'know', by a peculiar insight, what we ought to do on each and every occasion. Rather, practical insight is confined to basic deontic premisses and, from there on, we have to reason to more specific rules and, eventually, apply them to particular circumstances, both our reasoning and our applications being fallible in practical just as much as in theoretical matters. The central difficulty in this view is that it does not supply us with a method of identifying basic deontic propositions, since any two people may differ over which deontic propositions they claim to know by intuition.

It may here be objected, in Bonaventure's defence, that, unlike many modern intuitionists, he does have an independent criterion for basic deontic propositions, albeit a theological one, since he speaks, in this connection, of the law of God. His criterion might be that a deontic proposition is basic just in case it has been revealed by God. This cannot, however, be a correct exegesis, if only because no medieval theologian would ever have maintained that the truth of a revealed proposition is known to us innately, even in part. The point of revelation is precisely that it tells us what we should not otherwise have known, though it has also been held that, because of the fallibility of human reason, it also includes some things which we could, theoretically, work out for ourselves but in practice, because of the difficulty of the reasoning involved, often fail to do correctly. So Bonaventure might appeal to revelation in order to identify certain *derived* deontic propositions, but could not consistently do so in order to identify *basic* ones. Indeed, we have already seen that it is *natural* law which Bonaventure regards as being written in *conscientia*, so he must be using 'the law of God' as a synonym for this; and natural law, in medieval philosophy, is simply what is right or wrong independently of any legislation, the latter, by contrast, being termed 'positive' law and distinguished into divine and human.

The great majority of mankind is probably intuitionist in practice: most people think it is 'obvious' that certain kinds of action are right and others wrong, though perhaps more perplexity is to be found today than in former times. It is therefore of considerable importance to ask how an intuitionist position, even of the medieval type proposed by Bonaventure, might be justified. One way of identifying the basic deontic propositions would be to take them as the highest common factor of everybody's claimed intuitions. In a relatively homogeneous society, this solution has often been adopted unreflectively. Thus medieval writers are able to speak of the 'law of God' or of the 'natural law' as though it will be obvious to their readers what this comprises.

Even within the framework of western medieval society, though, how could an author like Bonaventure be confident that these shared intuitions were confined to *basic* deontic propositions? A certain deontic proposition may seem obvious to members of a given society because a suppressed non-deontic premiss is being taken for granted, and the former will not necessarily wear on its face the information that it is derivable from some other, more basic deontic proposition with the aid of a non-deontic assumption.

A topical example is the command in Genesis 1:28 to be fruitful and multiply and fill the earth. In the middle ages and, indeed, until very recently, this might have seemed to most people to yield a sure example of a basic deontic proposition, that reproduction (subject to certain provisos) should be maximised. Today we should ask for the point of the command, which appears to be the preservation of the human race. Given an under-populated world in which disease and unhygienic conditions produced a high mortality rate, preservation of the human race demanded that reproduction be maximised and, since these environmental conditions had prevailed since the earliest times, people can be forgiven for taking them for granted. Now that they have changed very dramatically, however, we can see that the proposition that reproduction ought to be maximised is a derived one. This is a particularly apposite example with which to confront Bonaventure, because it is parallel to his own about circumcision and diet: in both cases the non-deontic premiss was true, but is now false. Both examples also bring out very well that it is often only *after* a non-deontic premiss has changed its truth-value that we may recognise a deontic proposition as being derived rather than basic.

The highest common factor solution will thus have the result that the set of basic deontic propositions could vary from one time to another, its general tendency being to decrease in size. Moreover, in non-homogeneous societies like many today, it would be very much smaller than in medieval Europe while, if a global survey were required, it would be smaller still. Even in relatively homogeneous societies, it depends rather heavily upon turning a blind eye to minorities; the Catharists, for example, would not have shared many of Bonaventure's intuitions. But, in any case, a reflective intuitionist could hardly agree to an empirical method (the survey) for identifying basic deontic propositions, for what then becomes of the infallibility of *conscientia* in apprehending them, by a 'natural light' of reason, when no individual has any guarantee that his intuitions are genuine?

The alternative solution, put baldly, is for the intuitionist to claim that *he* (and perhaps his friends) has the genuine intuitions, the claimed intuitions of those who differ from him being mere pseudo-intuitions. Bonaventure certainly comes very close to this, in his answer to the question whether we are bound to do everything which *conscientia* tells us to be necessary to salvation:

Conscientia sometimes tells us what is in accordance with the law of God, sometimes what is in addition to the law of God and sometimes what is against the law of God . . . In the first case, *conscientia* binds without qualification . . . In the second case, *conscientia* binds so long as it persists, so that a man must either change his *conscientia* or must carry out what it tells him . . . In the third case, *conscientia* does not bind us to act or not to act, but binds us to change it . . . since such a *conscientia* is mistaken . . . It is therefore necessary to change it, since whether a man does what it says or the opposite, he sins mortally. For if he does what his *conscientia* tells him, and that is against the law of God, and to act against the law of God is mortal sin, then without any doubt he sins mortally. But if he does the opposite of what his *conscientia* tells him, the latter persisting, he still sins mortally, not in virtue of the deed which he does but because he does it in an evil way. For he does it in despite of God, so long as he believes, his *conscientia* telling him so, that this displeases God . . . The reason for this is that God does not merely take notice of *what* a man does, but with what intention he does it . . . (Translations, pp. 114–115).

The deontic propositions involved in the second and third cases envisaged in this passage are, *ex hypothesi*, derived and not basic, since *conscientia* is infallible, according to Bonaventure, in its apprehension of basic deontic propositions. These two cases, then, must always arise from mistakes in reasoning. Yet, in the third case, the man is caught in a double bind: not only can he do nothing right, but he cannot simultaneously persist in his deontic belief and recognise that he is bound to give it up; to recognise that his belief is false is *ipso facto* to change his *conscientia*. Now it would be inconsistent to allow that a man might get into this situation in good faith, since, if he were in good faith, he could not be hemmed in by mortal sin on every side. Consequently, his situation cannot just be the result of fallacious reasoning or a merely mistaken belief in a false non-deontic premiss; it must show, in addition, that he is depraved.

Bonaventure refrains from pressing his position to this conclusion, but it is nevertheless where the intuitionist road leads. Those who are confident that their intuitions are the genuine ones will then consider themselves justified in coercing, where they are able to do so, others who lay claim to intuitions which are incompatible with their own. It is a convenient licence, whose exercise is commonplace, for the oppression of minorities, and it is only where a group of minority intuitionists seize power that we really sit up and notice that intuitionism justifies, for its adherents, the worst species of tyranny, that of the tyrant who, far from paying no attention to his conscience, tyrannises in the name of conscience.

Faced with so many examples of this in history and especially in contemporary experience, the modern reaction is to abandon all attempt to justify deontic propositions, to regard conscience as a matter of belief rather than of knowledge, and to allow that there is no way of deciding between two sets of deontic beliefs, provided that each is internally consistent. From this it follows that any behaviour is to be tolerated which is in accordance with the agent's conscience, so long as it does not infringe the rights of others and, with this exception, that no one should ever try to persuade someone else to change his conscience, since *ex hypothesi* such persuasion could not be rational. The difficulties of this position are of no concern here, since no medieval philosopher ever held it; but there is a third alternative, relevant to the present topic, because it is latent in Bonaventure, though he confused it with intuitionism.

Bonaventure's argument that *conscientia* is partly an innate and partly an acquired disposition can be re-formulated in terms of *language*. It is partly acquired because, in order to formulate deontic propositions, one must first learn a language, for which perception and memory are necessary. Having learnt a language, however, some deontic propositions can be formulated whose truth can be determined without any further recourse to experience: in the terminology introduced later by Kant, they are *a priori*. We can then say that a deontic proposition is basic, in Bonaventure's sense, just in case it is both *a priori* and true. This is now a logical and no longer a psychological criterion for basic deontic propositions and is independent of whether we have any intuition about the truth of a deontic proposition.

That this is a possible interpretation of Bonaventure is supported by the parallel which he draws between basic deontic propositions and the theoretical proposition: 'every whole is greater than any of its parts'. Until very recently, it has been almost universal among philosophers to exaggerate the ease with which the truth-values even of theoretical *a priori* propositions may be determined. With the advent of Frege's logic, we now realise that the truth of some tautologies, to take the simplest and most straightforward example of *a priori* propositions, may not be at all obvious simply upon inspection; on the contrary, the proof may be quite difficult.

Moreover people's intuitions in these matters, except with the very simplest cases, are thoroughly unreliable. Bonaventure's assimilation of the *a priori* to the intuitively obvious is quite understandable, given the time at which he wrote, but today the two strands in his account must be sharply distinguished. Unfortunately, because he made this assimilation, Bonaventure did not see that it was necessary to pursue his investigation further and seek an appropriate method for determining the truth-values of *a priori* deontic propositions; thinking it complete, he turned to *synderesis*. *Synderesis*, for Bonaventure, is an innate tendency to want to do what is honourable rather than useful; this much we have already seen. In his second question on *synderesis*, he asks whether it can be extinguished by sin, replying that it cannot, though its exercise can temporarily be prevented:

> *Synderesis* is hampered by the darkness of blindness so that it does not murmur in reply to evil, because the evil is believed to be good, as e.g. in the case of heretics . . . Similarity, it is hampered by the wantonness of pleasure, for sometimes in sins of the flesh a man is so engrossed by the exercise of the flesh that a sense of guilt has no place, because men of the flesh are so far carried away by the impulse to pleasure that reason has then no place [in them]. *Synderesis* is also hampered by the hardness of obstinacy, so that it does not goad us into [doing] good, as e.g. in the case of the damned . . . (Translations, pp. 117–118).

The second of these three cases is at once reminiscent of the impulse to sin, so it is interesting that Bonaventure explicitly rejects any simple correspondence between *synderesis* and that impulse. In his first question on *conscientia*, he cites the argument: the law of the flesh is opposed to the law of the mind: but the law of the flesh is related to desire; so the law of the mind, i.e. *conscientia*, must also be related to desire. His reply is that although the law of the flesh consists mainly in a tendency of appetite to evil, it presupposes that imagination and apprehension represent bodily things to us in a disordered way and, hence, corruption of the perceptory potentiality which, of course, pertains to apprehension and not to desire (Translations, pp. 110–112). If we can assume that the law of the flesh is the same as the impulse to sin, Bonaventure thus sees it as having both an apprehensory component and a component relating to desire, very much in line with the rabbis. To the extent that the law of the mind can be regarded as its contrary, then, the latter will also have an apprehensory component (*conscientia*) and one relating to desire (*synderesis*).

Bonaventure also has a stronger reason for rejecting the correspondence, which develops a strand of thought which has already been noticed in Philip's treatise. The fourth argument which he cites to show that *synderesis* can be extinguished assumes the opposition, asserts that the impulse to sin can be totally extinguished, as, for example, in the Virgin Mary, and concludes that *synderesis* can also be extinguished. Bonaventure replies that they are not comparable, because the impulse to sin is not constitutive of human nature, whereas *synderesis* is; so the impulse to sin can be lost without affecting human nature, whereas *synderesis* cannot, nor, for that matter, *conscientia* (Translations, p. 118). Bonaventure thus plays down the impulse to sin as a guide, by analogy, to the nature of conscience, and it plays no significant role in his inquiry.

The first two cases in the passage quoted above of *synderesis* being prevented from operating lend little support to his view of it as a tendency of desire. For in both cases, according to him, *synderesis* cannot come into play because of a failure of *apprehension*. In the first, the apprehension is mistaken; in the second, it is temporarily thrust out of attention. It is only in the third that the idea of an independent tendency of desire gains any plausibility. What he has in mind is presumably the situation in which a person repeatedly acts against his conscience, until the point comes at which he no longer feels guilty about doing so. But the obstinate are those who, though wrong, are convinced that they are right, and the long-term effect of acting repeatedly against one's conscience is precisely to change it. At first, the pangs of guilt may be distressing. After a few repetitions, though, they will be felt less keenly, and the action seem less heinous. With further repetition, it will come to seem a mere peccadillo and occasion only the mildest twinge of regret. Meanwhile, reasons will be found to excuse the action, at least for the subject concerned. Finally, it will be seen in a new perspective in which it does not seem wrong at all. So here, too, there will be a change of apprehension. Bonaventure cites the damned as his example of obstinacy, but they regret their actions only because of the penalty incurred, which is quite different from being sorry because they believe that they have done *wrong*. Thus all three of his cases witness to a *conceptual* connection between believing that a certain kind of action is obligatory and a desire to perform it in appropriate circumstances. If a person has done something and really believes it to have been wrong, then he cannot but regret having done it, i.e. wish that he had not. The 'cannot' here has the force of logical consequence, which does not tally with Bonaventure's idea that one potentiality is involved in apprehending the action as wrong, but another in desiring that one had not done it.

The distinction which Bonaventure attempts to draw between *conscientia* and *synderesis* is thus unconvincing. His positive contribution to the analysis of conscience lies in his treatment of *conscientia*: first, in explicitly adopting the interpretation of deontic propositions as rules and, second, in developing the suggestion, already confusedly present in Philip's treatise, that some deontic propositions are necessary – for the *a priori* is one kind of necessity. It was a pity that he did not modify Philip's distinction, instead of essaying a completely new one, because he manifestly needs a distinction of that kind in order to mark out his basic deontic propositions from derived ones, whether or not the former are known by intuition or, rather, are identified by a logical criterion, for Bonaventure would be unable, without it, to give any straightforward answer to the question: 'Is his conscience right or wrong?' in just those cases which justify Philip's distinction.

4

Aquinas

Aquinas consolidated Philip's way of distinguishing between *synderesis* and *conscientia* with Bonaventure's notion of basic deontic propositions which are necessary, making the latter the proper objects of *synderesis*. He discussed conscience in three places: first, as one might expect, in his commentary on the *Judgements* of Peter Lombard, an early work of 1253–1255; second, in the sixteenth and seventeenth of his *Debated Questions on Truth*, which date from the academic session 1257–1258; and, finally, in the *Summa theologiae* 1.79, written about ten years later. The third discussion is indeed a summary of the second and, as he did not change his view in the meantime, I have taken the latter as the basis of my exposition. It also relates more closely to the texts which have already been considered here.

Aquinas, like Philip, begins with *synderesis*. His first question is the usual classificatory one: is it a potentiality or a disposition? Then, can it do wrong? and, to conclude, is it extinguished in some people? The argument by which Aquinas settles the first question is alien to a modern reader, because it involves a comparison of men with angels and presupposes a hierarchy of beings whose natures overlap:

a lower nature, at its highest, comes near to what is proper to a higher nature, participating in the latter imperfectly. Now the nature of the human mind is below that of an angel, if we consider what is the natural way for either to apprehend things. It is proper to the nature of an angel to apprehend the truth without inquiry or running over the matter, but proper to human nature to reach an apprehension of truth by inquiring and by running from one point to another. As a result, the human mind, at its highest, comes near to something of what is proper to an angelic nature, i.e. by apprehending some things immediately and without inquiry although, in this, it is inferior to an angel because it only apprehends the truth in such cases through the senses (Translations, p. 124).

He continues that angels have practical as well as theoretical apprehension, because they serve God in various spiritual offices, and thus

in human nature, in so far as it comes near to that of angels, there must be apprehension of the truth without inquiry both in theoretical and in practical matters.

Moreover, this apprehension must be the source of all subsequent apprehension, whether theoretical or practical, since sources should be more stable and certain. So this apprehension must be naturally present in man, because he apprehends it as a kind of seed-bed of all subsequent knowledge, just as the natural germs of subsequent behaviour and effects pre-exist in every nature. This apprehension must also be dispositional, so that it will be ready for use when needed.

Accordingly, just as there is a natural disposition of the human mind by which it apprehends the principles of theoretical disciplines, which we call the understanding of principles, so too it has a natural disposition concerned with the basic principles of behaviour, which are the general principles of natural law (Translations, p. 124).

The disposition in question, he concludes, is a disposition of the potentiality of reason, but *synderesis* can either be used to mean this disposition, which is comparable to that by which theoretical principles are apprehended, or to mean the potentiality of reason as endowed with this disposition.

Taking *synderesis* in the first sense, what is clear from this account is that Aquinas regards it as an innate rational disposition by which basic deontic premises are known to us without reasoning; so far, his view is the same as Bonaventure's, with a similar appeal to a practical counterpart of the Aristotelian model of an academic discipline, except that the labels are different: Aquinas' *synderesis* is part of Bonaventure's *conscientia*. Aquinas makes his position more precise in his replies to some of the arguments to the effect that *synderesis* is a potentiality which he cites at the beginning of this question. In particular, he clarifies the relationship of *synderesis* to the Augustinian distinction between higher and lower reason and to the impulse to sin.

In reply to the argument that *synderesis* is simply higher reason, because its objects are unchangeable (no. 9), he immediately spots an ambiguity in 'unchangeable' which Bonaventure missed:

a thing is said to be unchangeable because its nature is unchangeable; thus divine things are unchangeable. In this sense, higher reason aims at what is unchangeable. Something is also said to be unchangeable because of the necessity of its truth, although it is about things which are changeable with respect to their natures, e.g. the truth 'Every whole is greater than any of its parts' is unchangeable even in application [to changeable things]. In this sense, *synderesis* aims at what is unchangeable (Translations, p. 125).

The ambiguity could not have been more admirably expounded, but Aquinas is certainly making Augustine's distinction clearer than Augustine himself did. Indeed, he is re-defining it. Augustine's 'wisdom' and 'knowledge' are just Plato's 'knowledge' and 'belief' respectively; Augustine goes beyond Plato only in positing two parts of reason, a higher and a lower, to correspond to unchangeable and changeable objects of rational apprehension. According to the Platonic account, necessary propositions always concern the relationships of unchangeable things – the forms – so, for Plato (and Augustine), there could be no such distinction as Aquinas attempts to draw. Aquinas, however, follows Aristotle in rejecting separated forms, with the result that the range of unchangeable thing, is severely restricted (perhaps just to God and mathematical objects) and necessary propositions are by no means confined to the relationships between them. If Augustine had admitted a difference between necessary propositions and propositions about unchangeable things, it is a matter of conjecture which of the two he would have assigned as the objects of higher reason. Aquinas, in correlating higher reason with unchangeable objects, runs against the tide which washed the history of philosophy in the wake of Plato's original distinction: it was the fore-runner, rather, of the distinction between necessary and contingent propositions and, subsequently, between *a priori* and *a posteriori* ones. However, if we take higher reason as Aquinas expounds it, then it becomes irrelevant to conscience; as Aquinas concludes, *synderesis* then relates both to higher and to lower reason.

Instead of Augustine's distinction, Aquinas deploys an Aristotelian one in order to develop his account of how *synderesis* is related to reason. This derive from one of the most obscure and disputed passages in Aristotle, *De anima* 3.4–5, where he distinguishes between the active and the passive intellect. Aquinas had his own interpretation of this distinction, however, regarding it as marking off an active and a passive potentiality as being comprised in reason. He thinks that *synderesis* is a disposition of reason *qua* passive potentiality (16.1 *ad* 13) and, though he does not spell out his ground for this view, I think we can make a good guess at it. One of the prime examples of a passive potentiality is perception: seeing and hearing, for example, (in contrast to looking at and listening to) are things which happen to us rather than things which we do. Thus, in answer to the question: 'What are you doing?' I can reply 'I am looking at a man on the other side of the road.' Similarly, thinking out a problem or reasoning to a conclusion is doing something, but seeing (in the psychological sense) the point of an argument or that a certain proposition is true is to undergo something. Thus if *synderesis* is exercised in apprehension without inquiry, it will be an ability of the truth of certain deontic propositions to *strike* one: the very metaphor, as many of the others which we use in connection with insight, conveys passivity.

The opposition between *synderesis* and the impulse to sin is raised in two objections to his view which Aquinas considers. The first of these (no. 7) is that *synderesis*, as always inclining us to what is good, is opposed to sensuality, as always inclining us to what is evil; and, since sensuality is a potentiality without any disposition, so must *synderesis* be. The second (no. 11) is that contraries cannot be in the same thing, but there is an innate impulse to sin in us, which always inclines us to what is evil; so *synderesis*, which always inclines us to good, cannot be a disposition of the same potentiality and must, hence, be a potentiality in its own right. Aquinas replies to the former objection that sensuality always inclines us to evil only because of the impulse to sin, which is thus a disposition of sensuality, and to the latter that *synderesis* is a disposition of the higher part of the soul, i.e. reason, so that the impulse to sin is a disposition of a different potentiality from that of which *synderesis* is a potentiality.

He is thus able to uphold the opposition between the impulse to sin and *synderesis*, without getting into difficulties with his application of the potentiality/disposition distinction and, since perception is a potentiality of the 'lower part' of the soul, he can also accommodate Bonaventure's point that the impulse to sin carries a corruption of (perceptory) apprehension as well as of (non-rational) desire.

Aquinas' answer to the question whether *synderesis* can do wrong is, as the reader will by now expect, that it cannot. His reason, however, is not that it acts intuitively, but that the whole edifice of knowledge, whether theoretical or practical, rests upon basic principles, so that, if we could be wrong about these, nothing would be certain. This argument stands or falls with one's view of the edifice of knowledge; if it is not a deductive hierarchy, then the argument will not be convincing. But it does at least have the merit of transferring the field of dispute from the psychological to the logical, since Aquinas' criterion for basic deontic premisses is not that they are intuitively obvious, but that they are necessarily true. The question also affords him the opportunity to distinguish (in reply to objections 1 and 2) two ways in which a false conclusion is drawn from a basic deontic premiss: first, by fallacious inference; second, by combining it with some other premiss which is false (this, of course, does not *guarantee* a false conclusion). His example of the latter is those who killed the apostles, thinking that thereby they did God a service. This is very similar to Philip's example of the heretics who die for their beliefs, and does not warrant further discussion here, but there is one point in Aquinas' analysis which deserves mention. The basic deontic premiss from which these people argued, he says, is that we ought to serve God, and this is true. They combined it, however, with the premiss that killing the apostles would please God, and this is a false judgement of *higher* reason. This reveals Aquinas' motivation for not identifying *synderesis* with the practical side of higher reason.

He makes the same point in the second reply in his third question, this time apropos Philip's example of the heretics: they judge rightly that we ought to believe what God has said, but are mistaken about what God has said, again a false judgement of higher reason. On the question itself, whether *synderesis* can be extinguished, Aquinas has two new things to say. His solution is basically the same as Bonaventure's, that it cannot be extinguished but that it can be impeded in its operation. He claims that it cannot be extinguished, however, on the ground that it is in virtue of the light of *synderesis* that the soul is rational (together with the light by which basic theoretical premisses are known), i.e. that *synderesis* is constitutive of rationality. This is a large and very interesting claim. It can, of course, be interpreted in terms of intuition, to the effect that intuition, both theoretical and practical, is the distinguishing characteristic of rationality. But it can also be interpreted in terms of the necessary/contingent distinction, to the effect that the ability to formulate necessary (or *a priori*) thoughts and to recognise them as such is the distinguishing characteristic of rationality.

It is a great pity that Aquinas merely put forward this suggestion, almost as an aside, without following it up systematically, for the weakest aspect of the 2×2 matrix structure for the human soul is its horizontal division, between rational and non-rational. The vertical division, between the theoretical (apprehension) and the practical (desire) is strongly supported by many features of the behaviour of psychological verbs, but if all kinds of theoretical and practical reasoning are supposed to be the prerogative, among animals, of men, then it is awkward, to put it mildly, to account for some of the behaviour of the higher species of animals. Even Aquinas is forced to distinguish between two kinds of memory in order to allow other animals some kind of memory (*Summa theologiae* 1.79.6); if he had known what we now know about animal behaviour, he would have been faced with the necessity of similar duplications all along the line of psychological concepts.

In considering how the operation of *synderesis* can be obstructed,

Aquinas repeats the case in which a false conclusion is drawn from a basic deontic premiss or a deontic proposition is misapplied to particular circumstances. But he also adds a new case, where someone is deprived of free choice or of the use of reason, e.g. by injury to an organ of the body whose proper functioning is necessary to the use of reason. This would cover brain damage, and perhaps the effects of certain types of brain surgery such as leucotomy: it also allows for the thought disorder which is a characteristic mark of psychosis. Yet it is dubious whether detailed investigation of these examples would tally with Aquinas' picture of the situation, in which *synderesis qua* disposition is not lost, but the disposition can no longer be exercised. If a man who knows how to drive a car suffers paralysis as the result of a cerebral haemorrhage, he still knows how to drive even though he can no longer do so. But if he can no longer formulate basic deontic propositions, as a result of brain damage or psychosis, that is more closely comparable to blindness, which in Aristotelian and medieval terminology is a privation, i.e. a loss of the disposition, so that *synderesis* would be extinguished in him. This would not prevent Aquinas from holding that *synderesis* is constitutive of rationality, any more than cases of blindness force us to deny that perception is a potentiality belonging to the nature of animals.

Aquinas' treatment of *synderesis*, viewed as a whole, mainly consisted in a tidying-up operation. He grafted onto Philip's account some of Bonaventure's developments under the heading of *conscientia*, and clarified some ambiguities and distinctions. The few original features concern rather minor issues and, although he moved in the direction of making necessity the criterion of basic deontic propositions, it is still not clearly separated from intuition. The by then established tradition that *synderesis* is infallible was doubtless the major block to further clarification of this point. It was only when he turned to *conscientia* that Aquinas introduced some really new ideas. He raises five questions about *conscientia*: first, is it a potentiality, a disposition or an actualisation? second, can it be mistaken? third, are we bound by it? and, fourth, are we bound by a mistaken conscience? I shall not consider his fifth question here.

His answer to the first question comes as quite a surprise, for he holds that *conscientia* is an actualisation, on the ground that it consists in the *application* of knowledge to particular cases. He justifies this view, in the first instance, by recourse to linguistic analysis. This turns partly upon the double sense of '*conscientia*' as 'consciousness' as well as 'conscience' in the modern sense; to be conscious of something is to be aware of it, to be actually thinking about it. Moreover, he maintains that only this classification answers to all the ways we speak of conscience in everyday usage, e.g. 'I'll tell you what's on my conscience.' At this distance of time, it is no longer possible for us to judge whether Aquinas is giving an accurate account of the use of *'conscientia'* in thirteenth-century Latin, or whether it is a selective account which fits his own purposes, but we should certainly not obtain the same result from a survey of the use of 'conscience' in modern English, if for no other reason, then because 'conscience' embraces *synderesis* as well as *conscientia*. Thus, a man might say: 'It's against my conscience to fight in a war, but fortunately the situation has never arisen, so it hasn't been put to the test'; here he could just as well have said 'my principles' instead of 'my conscience'.

A second argument which Aquinas deploys is that the same word is only used for a potentiality, disposition and actualisation when there is only one way of actualising the potentiality or disposition. He instances 'sight', which can mean the ability to see or its exercise; but he also gives 'thought' (*'intellectus'*) as an example, whereas it seems to be, rather, a counter-example. All sorts of things count as thinking, and we have the vocabulary to specify them when needed: remembering something, pondering it, considering whether it is true, and so on. One's assessment of this example, however, turns to some extent upon the translation of *'intelligere'*, which is often rendered as 'understand' rather than as 'think'; thus *'cogitare'* would be used for thinking out a problem, not *'intelligere'*. On the other hand, Aquinas himself holds that *intellectus qua* potentiality is the same as reason (*Debated Questions on Truth* 15.1), so he cannot consistently maintain that there is only one use of *intellectus*, e.g. understanding.

As an example of a word which cannot mean a potentiality or a disposition, he cites 'use', since the use of something is *ipso facto* an actualisation; moreover, *any* potentiality or disposition can be used. It is difficult for us to come to grips with this suggestion, because there is no English verb corresponding to *'conscire'*, unless we fall back upon 'be conscious of', which relates to consciousness rather than to conscience. The point, presumably, is that the actualisation of any psychological potentiality or disposition involves bringing something to mind: we must be conscious of a piece of knowledge in order to use it, of a desire in order to be motivated by it, etc. I have already argued that this is, in general, false. Nor does conscience seem to be an exception: a man will often follow his conscience automatically, without calling to mind his principles and even perform an action without thinking, at the time, that it is an application of them, though that is how he would justify the action if challenged to do so afterwards.

However, the issue whether we always bring to mind basic deontic propositions in the course of applying them is probably only marginal. The essence of Aquinas' position is that we have a stock of such propositions, but that it remains to apply them. Given the Aristotelian scheme of classification into potentialities, dispositions and actualisations, and that the basic deontic propositions are part of our knowledge, it is a neat solution to say, first, that conscience does not constitute a distinct potentiality: second, that the stock of basic deontic propositions is a disposition of practical reason – call it *synderesis*: and, third, that the application of these propositions – call it *conscientia* – is the actualisation of that disposition. The way is then also open to maintaining that *synderesis* is never mistaken, but that *conscientia* may be so, since rules can always be misapplied.

This solution involves identifying the application of basic deontic propositions with the actualisation of our knowledge of them, and the difficulty which remains is whether this assimilation does not confine several distinct procedures, all of which can loosely be termed 'applications', within an Aristotelian strait-jacket which over-simplifies the situation to the point of misrepresentation. To do him justice, Aquinas recognises two distinct applications of *synderesis*:

In one, we are directed through the disposition of knowledge to do or not to do something. In the other, the actualisation is tested, after it has taken place, by the disposition of knowledge, for whether it be right or not right. These two forms of application correspond to two in theoretical matters, viz. to discovery and judgement. The form by which, through knowledge, we look at what should be done, as though taking advice, is comparable to discovery, by which we track down conclusions from premisses. But the form by which we test and discuss whether what has already occurred is right, is comparable to judgement, by which conclusions are traced back to premisses (Translations, p. 131).

He is clearly right to distinguish the case in which a person asks himself the question before acting, 'What ought I to do?', from that in which, afterwards, he asks himself: 'Did I do the right thing?' But the parallel with theoretical reasoning which he draws is confusing rather than explanatory. To be sure, in asking 'What ought I to do?' I am trying to find out, i.e. discover, what to do, and in asking 'Did I do the right thing?' I am trying to form a judgement upon my action. In theoretical reasoning, however, the situation is not parallel, but reverse.

Theoretical discovery does *not* consist in drawing conclusions from premisses; rather, we look at the facts and try to find an explanation for them, which often takes the form of a theory, i.e. a set of premisses, from which they follow as conclusions. And that is like looking for a justification of one's action. The theoretical analogue of 'What ought I to do?' is *prediction*, where we draw conclusions from our theories and then test them against the facts. Aquinas has been misled, here, by Aristotle's model of an academic discipline; the inverse relationship between theoretical and practical reasoning has been developed recently by Kenny (1975, chap. 5).

However, this distinction, even when the comparison with theoretical reasoning is corrected, does not touch the ambiguity in the notion of *applying* or *actualising* deontic knowledge which is introduced by differentiating between basic and derived deontic propositions. Aquinas is silent about the procedure by which *derived* deontic propositions are obtained. This will, indeed, involve drawing conclusions from basic deontic premisses (with the aid of other, non-deontic ones), but the resulting derived deontic propositions may not be for immediate use; they may not be answers to the question 'What ought I to do *now*?' but, rather, to the question: 'What ought I to do if at some time or other I find myself in such-and-such a type of circumstance?' They are dispositional just as much as the basic ones and, even after deducing them, the 'What ought I to do now?' question can still arise, when the issue is whether a derived deontic proposition applies to given circumstances. Both Bonaventure and Aquinas, indeed, recognise this, as we have seen from some of their examples, in which the derived deontic conclusions are themselves rules, which may not find any immediate application.

Moreover, in both theoretical and practical matters, justification is usually more difficult than deduction. Given a set of premisses, it is relatively easy to determine what, if anything, may validly be deduced from them: there are methods of proof, and decision procedures. By contrast, there is no systematic method of finding premisses which will justify a proposition given as a putative conclusion. Experience supports this in the practical as well as the theoretical sphere: armed with some rather general and wide-ranging rules, and a knowledge of the world, we have little difficulty in deducing more specific rules (even though our deductions may not always be valid), whereas the justification of deontic propositions is usually extremely difficult. When it comes to the *application* of rules, however, the boot is on the other foot; because of the connection between conscience and the emotions, people feel guilty when they act against their principles and the emotion draws their attention to the discrepancy even when, before the deed, they may be rather unsure about what to do.

The two kinds of application which Aquinas distinguishes are thus not the appropriate ones in the context of his question. What he needs is, rather, a distinction, in the first instance, between two *uses* of deontic propositions and it would have been better, in order to avoid confusion, not to call the first, which is to deduce further deontic propositions, an application at all. The second use consists in applying (or perhaps mis-applying) the rule to particular circumstances; this may consist in an action, but may also consist in formulating an intention to act in a certain way on a specific, foreseen occasion. Both of these uses will belong to *conscientia* and not to *synderesis* on Aquinas' reckoning; Aristotle's category of actualisation fails to distinguish them.

Aquinas' second question on *conscientia* is whether it can be mistaken. The greater part of his reply is predictable. It can be mistaken in two ways: either through the combination of a basic deontic premiss with another, false premiss, or through invalid reasoning. There is the same failure as in the previous question to distinguish these mistakes from misapplication of a rule, and the assimilation is shown very clearly by Aquinas' description of basic deontic propositions as general premisses, the conclusions drawn from them being described as particular. There is no advance, here, on Bonaventure's treatment. But Aquinas concludes by remarking that there is one case in which *conscientia* is infall-ible, when the particular conclusion 'falls directly' under the universal premiss. His examples are 'God is not to be loved by me' and 'Some-thing bad ought to be done'. The general premisses under which these fall are, presumably, 'I ought to love God' and 'One ought not to do anything bad' respectively. If so, then they are merely negated trans-formations of the premisses, the first a passive transformation and the second involving, in addition, an interchange of quantifiers with appro-priate modifications of negation. These examples are rather surprising, because what we should have expected from his description 'falling directly' under the general premiss is an example like 'One ought not to tell a lie; to say such-and-such in these circumstances would be a lie; therefore I ought not to say that in these circumstances'. It is also un-clear why he thinks that no one can make a mistake in such transforma-tions; as a matter of experience people can and do, especially where the premiss contains multiple quantification.

His failure to cite the kind of example we should expect, however, suggests an explanation for his assimilation of the two uses of a rule distinguished above. Is my example about lying one of applying a rule or of deducing a derived rule? Aquinas would probably have answered 'both', and add that it is precisely such cases which justify him in not distinguishing deduction from application. The application, however, consists in bringing saying what was in question under the description 'telling a lie'. This is already embodied in the second premiss, so the example is one of a simple deduction, consisting in the elimination of universal quantifiers. The conclusion is still a rule. It is not restricted, in its application, to a single occasion, since 'these circumstances' will be specified by a description which, in principle, could be satisfied on subsequent occasions. Because Aquinas is still aligning rule and application with general and particular, though, with no exact exposition of the latter distinction, he assimilates derived rules to applications of a rule and, since he allows that rules can be misapplied, he cannot instance simple deductions of the type which I have given as an example as those in which we cannot make a mistake.

Aquinas' most important and original contributions to the medieval debate about conscience are made in his answer to the third question on *conscientia*, whether it binds us. He says immediately that it does, but goes on to explain *how* it does so:

'binding', used of spiritual things, is a metaphor taken from bodily ones, which implies the imposition of necessity . . . There are two kinds of necessity which can be imposed by another agent. The first is a necessity of force, through which everything absolutely necessarily has to do what is determined by the action of the agent; the other should not strictly be called force but, rather, inducement. This is a conditional necessity, that is, deriving from a goal; e.g. there may be a necessity imposed upon someone that, if he does not do such-and-such, he will not obtain his reward.

. . . The second kind of necessity can be imposed upon the will, e.g. it may be necessary to choose such-and-such, if a certain good is to result, or if a certain evil is to be avoided . . . But just as the necessity of force is imposed on bodily things by some action, so conditional necessity is imposed upon the will by some action. The action by which the will is changed, however, is the command of a ruler or governor . . . But the action of a bodily agent only introduces necessity into another thing by its forceful contact with the thing on which it acts; so someone is only bound by the command of a ruler or lord, too, if the command reaches him who is commanded; and it reaches him through knowledge.

Hence no one is bound by any injunction except by means of knowledge of that injunction and, therefore, anyone who is not capable of being informed, is not bound by the command; nor is someone who is ignorant of an injunction of God bound to carry out the injunction, except in so far as he is obliged to know the injunction (Translations, pp. 133–134).

At a first reading, the content of this reply may appear to belong to the philosophy of mind. It distinguishes psychological from physical necessity and then goes on to explain how psychological necessity works. But it also belongs to the theory of meaning, for we can take it as an exposition of the meaning of 'ought' in deontic propositions. Indeed, it is now commonplace that there is a close, though not exact, analogy between 'obligatory' and 'necessary' on the one hand, and 'permissible' and 'possible' on the other; this is reflected in the way we sometimes say 'must' instead of 'ought', e.g. 'One must not tell a lie'. Thus interpreted, Aquinas' first contention is that deontic propositions are to be expounded as implicit conditionals. He is aligning the meaning of 'ought' in the deontic propositions with which ethics is concerned with its meaning in a much wider range of contexts, those in which it introduces a necessary *means* to a *goal*. The goal is given in the antecedent of the conditional, e.g. 'If you want to be in London by ten tomorrow morning, then you ought to take the seven-thirty train at the latest'. Often, the goal is presupposed and so we do not bother to state it; given that the context is known, it might be quite enough to say to the man envisaged in the last example: 'You ought to take the seven-thirty train.'

What, then, is the presupposed goal in ethical contexts? To Aquinas, this presents no difficulty: it is obedience to God's commands. Aquinas is most explicit about this in his answer to the question whether a mistaken conscience binds:

it does not seem possible for someone to escape sin if his *conscientia*, however much mistaken, tells him that something is an injunction of God which is indifferent or bad *per se* and, such *conscientia* remaining, he arranges to do the contrary. For so far as in him lies, by this itself he has the wish that the law of God be not observed; hence he sins mortally (Translations, p. 135).

This passage must be read very carefully: Aquinas does *not* hold the view, often to be found in modern authors, that it is always wrong to act against one's conscience, as such. First, let us remind ourselves that he is talking only about *conscientia* and not about *synderesis*: in his view, a man *cannot* be mistaken about basic deontic propositions. So the sense in which the man envisaged has a mistaken conscience is either that he has drawn a false deontic conclusion from his stock of basic deontic propositions or that he has misapplied a deontic proposition to particular circumstances. Nevertheless, the man in question thinks that God enjoins upon him a certain type of action or a particular action. But his desire to obey the law of God will be a concomitant of his belief – for

Aquinas, his knowledge – that God ought to be obeyed, and this, being a basic deontic proposition, will belong to *synderesis* and not to *conscientia*. So it is not because he acts against his *conscientia* that he does wrong but because, in acting against his *conscientia*, he is also acting against his *synderesis*, which is infallible.

Even within the context of his own account of conscience, Aquinas' explanation of the way in which *conscientia* binds only transposes the difficulty. For, if the presupposed antecedent is 'you want to obey God's commands', and we then ask *why* a person wants to do so, the answer will presumably be because he believes (or knows) that he *ought* to obey God's commands. So now we have to explain the meaning of this 'ought'. Moreover, once committed to an explanation of the meaning of 'ought' in terms of necessary means to a goal, we are not at liberty to switch to a totally different type of explanation at this point, for, if we did so, 'ought' here would have a different meaning from that which it bears in other deontic propositions and thus they could not be validly deduced from it. The only way in which the explanation can terminate is thus by positing a goal which calls for no further justification, i.e. an *a priori* goal.

Implicitly, Aquinas gives his answer to this difficulty when he argues that the way in which *conscientia* binds us is a special case of the way in which we are bound by the commands of a ruler, namely, by the threat of sanctions for disobedience or promise of a reward for obedience: 'e.g. there may be a necessity imposed upon someone that, if he does not do such-and-such, he will not obtain his reward'. God being the ruler *par excellence*, his rewards and sanctions are then the ultimate ones. It is not the place here to urge the theological objections to this solution, but it is pertinent to inquire whether it can survive 'secularisation', i.e. whether anything remains if we take account of those who do not believe in the existence of God or, at least, in a god who is the ultimate ruler and dispenser of rewards and punishments. They, too, appear to have consciences, so an account of conscience which does not provide for them will be unsatisfactory even to one who shares Aquinas' theological beliefs.

Wittgenstein remarked that following a rule is *analogous* to obeying an order, but he did not go so far as to make it a *special case* of obeying an order (1953, I. 206). Two aspects of the analogy are relevant here. First, as Aquinas argues, I have to know the rule in order to follow it and the command in order to obey it. It would not be enough that someone else, watching my behaviour over a period of time, observed a regularity in it which would be explained if I were following a rule or obeying a command; that might just be accidental, or I might have been following some rule or obeying some command other than the one which he invoked to explain my behaviour. The other relevant feature of the analogy is that the *point* of a rule or command lies outside itself. We give people commands in order to get things done, to change the world so that it conforms to our wishes; commands are means to goals, though the goals are those of the people who give the commands rather than of those who execute them. Similarly, one does not – at least, normally – follow a rule just for the sake of doing so. Even in following the rules of a game, which are arbitrary outside the context of the game, we follow them because we want to play the game. This adds weight to Aquinas' contention that 'ought' introduces a necessary means to a goal. Children sometimes walk along a pavement so as to avoid stepping on cracks between the paving-stones; here, exceptionally, they may be following a rule for its own sake – just for a bit of fun. But who would want to say that people follow their consciences in this spirit?

Well, do people have an end-in-itself in mind when they follow their consciences? We are concerned here, of course, with how they would *justify* their deontic beliefs, not with behaviour that is just a result of training and the internalisation of deontic beliefs which they have not scrutinised. I think they do, though in one sense it may not be the same goal for everyone. We all form for ourselves some conception of what a good life consists in, where 'good life' does not *mean* 'a life conducted in accordance with our deontic beliefs' but something more like 'a life which will make us happy in the long run'. At first, no doubt, we absorb this conception from our mentors, but later modify it in the light of our own experience. The religious man's conception of what a good life consists in will, of course, be very different from that of the agnostic or atheist, so it is only as long as we keep the level of description of the ultimate goal as 'a good life' that it is the same for everyone. Thus, the necessary means to achieving it will also differ from person to person, and these will constitute their deontic beliefs (or would do so, if people were consistent).

We have already seen that Aquinas holds that a mistaken *conscientia* is, in general, binding, but not how he deals with the case in which a man believes that he is obliged to do something where the action in question is evil. His view about this case is slightly more lenient, but only slightly, than Bonaventure's. If the mistake is not itself sinful, e.g.

when it arises from some factual mistake, then the man who follows his mistaken *conscientia* is excused; but if the mistake is one of law, then he is not excused, any more than a plea of ignorance of the law excuses in the courts (17.4 *ad* 5), because the mistake has arisen from ignorance of something he ought to have known (17.4 *ad* 3). Aquinas realises that, in this situation, whatever a man does will be wrong and that, *prima facie*, it appears to be contradictory: he is obliged to ϕ and he is obliged not to ϕ. However, he argues that, on closer consideration, it is a case of 'if *p*, then *q*; but not *q*', which is not a contradiction. As a parallel example, he cites a man who is bound to give alms to someone, but does so with an intention of vainglory: if that is his intention, then he is obliged not to give the alms, but *ex hypothesi* he is obliged to give them. The dilemma can be resolved quite simply by giving up the bad intention. Similarly here: if he believes that he is obliged to ϕ, then he is obliged to ϕ; but he is obliged not to ϕ. So the solution is for him to give up his belief that he is obliged to ϕ (17.4 *ad* 8). It is an ingenious answer, but no more convincing than and, indeed, no real advance upon Bonaventure's, for the difficulty still remains that a man who believes that he is obliged to ϕ will not simultaneously recognise that he is obliged not to ϕ and so will not see *himself* as being in a dilemma, while, the moment he does recognise it, he will have given up his belief that he is obliged to ϕ.

Yet Aquinas does allow that a mistaken *conscientia* excuses *except* where we can say that the person ought to have known better, and he does not justify his position that a man who is mistaken about a matter of law, i.e. about a deontic proposition, can never be mistaken in good faith. It is seldom that the opportunity arises to cite Aristotle in order to confute Aquinas, but Aristotle remarks, apropos the law courts, 'We punish those who are ignorant of anything in the laws that they ought to know *and that is not difficult*' (*Nicomachean Ethics* 3.5,1113^{b}23–27). Now basic deontic propositions are not in question for Aquinas here, because *synderesis*, according to him, cannot be mistaken. Hence the objects of a mistaken *conscientia* must always be false *derived* deontic propositions or else misapplications of deontic propositions. But the former, on his own admission, can arise only from fallacious reasoning or from the use of false non-deontic premisses. Moreover, the latter would not count as ignorance of fact in the sense in which he is contrasting it with ignorance of law; ignorance of fact in this legal sense is concerned with mistaken descriptions of circumstances to which a law is *applied*. Deriving conclusions from premisses often *is* difficult to do correctly, whether in theoretical or practical matters, so what right has Aquinas to impute evil to everyone who believes false *derived* deontic propositions?

Unwittingly, perhaps, Aquinas laid the foundations of an argument which could lead to a much more lenient position than he himself envisaged. For if there are relatively few basic deontic propositions, then the scope for a mistaken *conscientia* which is in good faith will be correspondingly wide. It then becomes important for us to identify the basic deontic propositions, and it is one of the most remarkable features of the medieval treatment of conscience, in view of the central role of the *synderesis/conscientia* distinction, that no serious attempt to do this was ever made. But there is a nasty twist at the end of this train of thought. Aquinas maintains that a mistaken conscience is binding on the ground that 'We ought to obey God's commands' is a basic deontic proposition; if it is not, then at least some alternative meta-rule must be shown to be basic in order to maintain that a mistaken conscience can *ever* excuse. Otherwise, we have not the slightest ground to suppose that there is a valid consequence from 'A believes that he ought to ϕ' to 'A ought to ϕ', any more than from 'A believes that p' to 'p'. In that case, the right advice to give to someone who has a mistaken conscience is to act against it and disregard any feelings of guilt. The only *exception* will be the religious man, when he believes that what he thinks he ought to do is commanded by God!

5

Balance-sheet

It is sometimes said that there is no progress in philosophy but, although philosophical progress differs in many respects from that in other disciplines, the medieval discussion of conscience shows that the notion is not entirely inapplicable to philosophy, too. For, on the one hand, there is a clearly discernible development in the thought of the three authors whose work on conscience has been studied here while, on the other, there are aspects of the topic to which we should be sensitive today to which they were blind. At this stage, it is worth drawing up a balance-sheet itemising the credits and debits which may be assigned to them.

The first item to be recorded is the surprising lack of attention which they pay, when we consider that they were professional theologians as well as philosophers, to biblical material on conscience. Of the texts which a modern biblical scholar would discuss were he writing on this topic (cf. e.g. Davies, 1962; Pierce, 1953), very few are cited by Philip, Bonaventure or Aquinas and even fewer play more than an incidental role in their arguments. Whether we assign this to the credit or to the debit side of the account will depend upon our point of view, but it has at least the result that a great deal of their discussion is accessible to philosophers who do not share their theological beliefs.

I have argued that the distinction between *synderesis* and *conscientia*, as expounded by Philip and developed by Aquinas, belongs to the credit column. This calls for two qualifications, however, for the distinction can be taken both logically and psychologically and the three medieval authors tend, on the whole, to mix psychology with logic. As a logical distinction, it is one between the *objects* of conscience, namely, deontic thoughts, which are expressed by different types of deontic proposition. Philip's attempt to align it with general versus particular deontic propositions must be accounted unsatisfactory, but Bonaventure made the requisite correction when he saw, however confusedly, that the relevant difference lay between necessary and contingent deontic propositions.

This provides several lines of enquiry for philosophers today. The medievals, admittedly, did not establish that there *are* any *a priori* deontic propositions but, if we once grant the notion of a deontic *proposition*, it would not be surprising if, as with non-deontic propositions, there are *a priori* as well as *a posteriori* ones. We should want to subdivide any search for the former by Kant's other distinction, between analytic and synthetic propositions, because a different method for establishing the status of the proposition is appropriate to each. If there are any analytic *a priori* deontic propositions, then their truth or falsity will be determined by the *meanings* of the expressions which they contain. Here Aquinas provides the cue: we have to explain the meaning of 'ought' and, if he is right, this will involve an analysis of the correlative notions *means* and *goal*.

At the other end of the spectrum, we might now have to distinguish between two types of synthetic *a posteriori* deontic proposition. The medievals have already drawn our attention to one group, those which are derivable from *a priori* deontic propositions together with other, non-deontic *a posteriori* propositions. Their distinction between basic and derived deontic propositions is of the utmost consequence because it provides a rational basis for explaining, and justifying, ethical change. Many people find it a difficulty that what is right in one generation might be wrong in another and conversely; within limits, however, this may actually be imposed upon us if we are to remain consistent, for, if factual premises which have hitherto been combined with *a priori* deontic propositions to yield deontic conclusions should cease to be true, new conclusions may follow from the *a priori* premises and these could even be inconsistent with the old conclusions. If we do not give up the old conclusions, we shall then be forced to abandon the very *a priori* premises on which they rested. In order to decide what can change in ethics and what cannot, however, it will be essential to identify any *a priori* deontic propositions and, by contrast, derived ones.

Aquinas does notice, elsewhere, certain cases in which changed circumstances either do or could call for corresponding ethical change. First, he draws an interesting distinction between deriving deontic propositions by deduction and by *specification* (*Summa theologiae* 2–1.95.2 *co*). A modern example of specification would be the rule of the road: public safety demands that we either have a rule to drive on the left, or a rule to drive on the right, but the necessity for having *some* rule of the road does not determine for which of the two any society should opt. Second, he considers the change from the polygamy allowed under the Mosaic law to the Christian demand for monogamy, but justifies this in terms of a distinction between primary and secondary ends of an activity, changes in the latter being possible provided that the primary end is respected (*Summa theologiae*, supplement, 65.1 *co*; 65.2 *co*). But although these cases are closely related to the point at issue, they are distinct from it, since we are concerned here with deontic propositions derived by deduction and are not restricted to activities in respect to which a distinction between primary and secondary ends may be discerned.

The possibility of a second group of synthetic *a posteriori* deontic propositions was not considered by medieval philosophers, but could there not be some deontic propositions whose truth rests upon experience? Of course, this will not be experience in the same sense as the experience by reference to which non-deontic synthetic *a posteriori* propositions are verified or falsified. Perception, for example, would not be to the point. In most societies, though, older people have been recognised as a source of deontic wisdom, not because they have devoted their lives to identifying and proving analytic *a priori* deontic propositions, but because they have tested rules of behaviour through their experience of life and of human relationships. It is only as a tentative suggestion that I put forward this idea of a second group of *a posteriori* deontic propositions, though, because there still remains the possibility of synthetic *a priori* ones. *Ex hypothesi* the truth-values of the latter could not be established either by an analysis of meaning or by empirical methods, but only by transcendental arguments: arguments, that is to say, that our experience *could* not be what it is unless they were true. It may be just this kind of argument which underlies an elder's claim that he or she has come to recognise the truth (or falsity) of some deontic proposition through long experience of life and people.

The second qualification that is necessary is to separate the range of problems just surveyed from those connected with the *application* of rules, whether *a priori* or *a posteriori* and whether basic or derived. Wittgenstein's pioneering discussion of what is involved in following a rule (1953, 1.85–243) has not, so far, been quarried for ethics; I have drawn upon it above, but have far from exhausted the quarry. In particular, his discussion is relevant to the question how we acquire deontic beliefs.

There is nothing in the distinctions between the objects of conscience which demands corresponding psychological distinctions; in one way,

Bonaventure was right to depart from Philip's precedent. It is only when the further assumption is made that we cannot be mistaken about the truth-values of *a priori* propositions that psychological implications are introduced. Although I have argued that this assumption is false, the strength of the medieval tradition that *synderesis* is infallible witnesses to a motivation that probably goes deeper than the texts acknowledge. Indeed, it is this part of the medieval theory of conscience which, more than any other, has filtered down to the present. In its religious form, it persists in the notion of conscience as the voice of God speaking within us, which is quite explicit, for example, in the following passage from Newman:

That inward light, given as it is by God, ... was intended to set up within us a standard of right and truth; to tell us our duty in every emergency, to instruct us in detail what sin is, to judge between all things which come between us, to discriminate the precious from the vile, to hinder us from being seduced by what is pleasant and agreeable, and to dissipate the sophisms of our reason (1849, pp. 89–90).

This is the final flowering of Basil's notion of conscience as a natural tribunal (cf. notes on the translations, 6, p. 77). In its secular form, it persists in the view that, so long as a man acts in accordance with his conscience, no evil can be imputed to him.

The medievals were preserved from these excesses by their distinction between *synderesis* and *conscientia*; but why were they so anxious to maintain that *synderesis*, at least, is infallible? The answer, I suspect, is that their underlying motivation was theological, deriving from a widely influential passage by St Paul:

When Gentiles who do not have the law do by nature what the law requires, they are a law to themselves, even though they do not have the law. They show that what the law requires is written on their hearts, while their conscience also bears witness and their conflicting thoughts accuse or perhaps excuse them on that day when, according to my gospel, God judges the secrets of men by Christ Jesus (Romans 2:15–16).

This is one of the prime sources for the medieval notion of natural law and, as we have seen, there is a strong tendency among medieval writers to identify the objects of *synderesis*, in Philip's and Aquinas' sense, with the natural law. That it is 'written on their hearts' suggests, moreover, both an external source, so that it is the voice of God speaking within them, and that it is innate, so that they cannot be mistaken about it. But if we look at the passage more closely, this exegesis is less convincing, for, in its context, St Paul is speaking of the Mosaic law and is careful to introduce his remark with the qualification: 'When Gentiles do by nature what the law requires'. Even a cursory reading of Romans 1-2 should be enough to persuade one that St Paul does not by any means suppose that this condition is always, or even for the most part, fulfilled. Like us, St Paul lived in an ethically heterogeneous society; the medieval interpretation of what he says here could only seem plausible because western medieval society was, ethically, largely homogeneous.

The failure of medieval philosophers to recognise that people's deontic beliefs are, for the most part, formed by training, must appear to us a major item on their debit account. Yet this can be regarded, not as a major defect in their account of conscience but, rather, as restricting the scope of their enquiry. Although they do not always keep psychology distinct from logic, the focus of their interest, throughout, is logical. The formation of conscience through training is primarily a question for psychology, and the medieval inquiry into conscience falls into place if we regard it as restricted to reflective conscience, i.e. to the conscience of an adult who has reflected upon the deontic beliefs in which he was brought up and has attempted to justify, at least to himself, those which he has retained or has subsequently adopted. Perhaps few people carry out this reassessment of their deontic beliefs thoroughly and systematically, but most of us, especially in these times, reconsider, in adolescence or adulthood, some of the principles of behaviour in which we were trained. The medieval inquiry rests upon an idealisation in this regard, but that is perfectly reasonable if the question at issue is the logical and epistemological status of deontic propositions.

In rejecting the view that we cannot be mistaken about the truth-values of *a priori* deontic propositions, we are not committed to excluding the possibility of deontic knowledge. On the contrary, we increase the scope for deontic knowledge, for it is dubious, in cases where there is no room for mistake, whether we can properly speak of knowledge at all (cf. Wittgenstein, 1969). What is the point of claiming that we know something if no one *can* be mistaken about it? Of course, if someone *is* mistaken, then he does not know it, but merely believes it and, perhaps, also believes (falsely) that he knows it. It is much more difficult to determine when a man knows something as against holding a true belief, but that is a problem which extends to theoretical belief and knowledge as much as to practical, and so is not restricted to conscience. We can at least say, though, that a man knows something if he can establish its truth by a valid argument, so the way is open to giving a place to *a priori* deontic knowledge. Yet the difference between knowledge and belief does not appear to relate to a distinction of potentialities: we could not imagine a species whose members were able to believe things but never to know anything.

The psychologically interesting aspect of conscience is that it involves our emotions as well as our reason. Of the three authors considered here, Bonaventure was the only one who attempted to integrate this into his account, and it is perhaps more important that he saw the problem than that he was unable to solve it satisfactorily. The phenomenon of guilt, *qua* emotion, is the ground for maintaining that there is a valid consequence from schema (S3) or schema (S4) to (S5). Medieval philosophers were more interested in guilt in the non-psychological than in the psychological sense, but Aquinas, for example, seems to have regarded guilt *qua* emotion as a kind of sorrow or sadness (*Summa theologiae* 2–1.39.2 *ad* 3). To the extent that a man feels guilty about something that he has done, he is sorry or sad that he did it. Well, to be sorry that one ϕed is the same as regretting that one ϕed which, in turn, is equivalent to wishing that one had not ϕed. In the case of feeling guilty, the ground for wishing that one had not ϕed is that one believes that one ought not to have ϕed and so, transposing this *ante factum*, a person who believes that he ought to ϕ will *ipso facto* wish to ϕ.

This logical connection between conscience and desire sits awkwardly upon the 2 × 2 matrix classification of psychological potentialities. *Qua* knowledge or belief it must be accounted a kind of apprehension, yet it also engages desire. There are, indeed, other logical connections between apprehension and desire. Thus many emotions entail certain beliefs. The emotion which concerns us here, sadness, is a typical example: if a man is sad that p, then he believes that p. Connections of this type did not escape the attention of medieval philosophers. They dealt with them by saying that we must first apprehend something before it can become an object of desire (or aversion), i.e. that there is a progression from apprehension to desire. The special interest of the connection between conscience and guilt, however, is that it goes the other way round: the desire is a necessary condition of the apprehension, not the apprehension of the desire.

We are familiar, today, with other examples of this reverse connection: the way, for example, that our emotions and expectations can sometimes distort our perception. But we tend, at any rate, to think of most of these reverse connections as more or less pathological, and certainly not as *logical* connections. Conscience is thus exceptional; the nearest parallel to the other pathological cases which it exhibits occurs with *irrational guilt*. We speak of irrational guilt in two senses: first, when a person feels guilty in the normal way because he believes that he ought not to have done something, yet has done it, but the belief is false. I am not concerned with this sense here. The other case typically arises when a person has *changed* his deontic belief on some point, but feels guilty when he acts in accordance with his new belief, as though he still held the old one. This suggests that deontic beliefs (and perhaps other beliefs too) operate at two levels, one at which they receive our conscious assent, the other at which they are actually operative in our conduct. If the two levels are not in harmony, then the result is a conflict of desires.

Irrational guilt in this sense did not come within the medieval purview. Today, it is certainly one of the phenomena which would have to be investigated in order to elucidate the connection between apprehension and desire involved in conscience, so it is not surprising that Bonaventure was unable to solve the problem which he raised. If medieval writers had been more aware of irrational guilt, though, they would doubtless have seen it as central to their concerns, because the problem of chronic conflicts of desires, from which their inquiry began, may be closely related to it. We find it difficult to take entirely seriously the professed deontic beliefs of a man who quite regularly acts against them, more especially when, as often happens, such chronic conflicts are found in otherwise highly conscientious, even scrupulous people. 'He can't *really* believe that what he does is so wrong', we are tempted to say. But what is the force of 'really' here, if not the suggestion, again, that beliefs operate at two different levels? Moreover, there seem to be only two long-term solutions to these conflicts. One consists in a change of professed belief in order to bring it into line with conduct, a quite appropriate solution where the professed belief cannot be justified. The other, of which conversion experiences, Augustine's among them, are clear examples, is a deeper conviction which becomes effective in regulating conduct. Yet chronic conflicts of desires differ from irrational guilt in that the guilt which accompanies them matches the professed belief, not the operative one, and, to this extent, the professed belief is not just a sham, but has to be taken seriously.

This is not the only respect in which the medieval analysis of chronic conflicts of desires was inadequate. All three of the authors whose work on conscience has been discussed here see them as conflicts between reason and bodily appetites. Because conscience is always on the side of reason, the impulse to sin is linked to bodily appetites. We can see *why* they saw chronic conflicts of desires in this restricted way: it fitted in so neatly with so many other ideas which they had inherited – the rabbinic doctrine of the two impulses, the Platonic distrust of the material world and search for wisdom through contemplation of eternal truths, the classificatory scheme of Aristotle's philosophy of mind and, indeed, certain aspects of Christianity. It is probable, too, that in Europe the chronic conflicts of desires of which people have been most conscious are those created by bodily and especially sexual appetites.

Yet there are also other, more subtle examples of chronic conflicts of desires which may be more fundamental to human nature. One example is the desire for psychological security, which is manifested especially in a craving for respect from our fellow-men: to what lengths will people not go in order to secure this respect? Sometimes they will be prepared to sacrifice one kind of respectability for the sake of another, which is more important in the eyes of their acquaintances, so the quest for respectability can take many different forms. It is almost certain, though, to come into conflict with conscience on one issue or another and, in nine cases out of ten, the conflict is eventually resolved in favour of respectability, conscience being changed to accord with it. This is often what we are describing when we speak of the idealism of youth being tempered by experience of the world.

The desire for respectability is by no stretch of the imagination a bodily appetite; it can frequently even be a curb to pleasure-seeking. It is also a peculiarly human characteristic, so that, if we were to try to fit it into the 2×2 matrix classification of the structure of the soul, it would have to be accounted a rational desire. This brings out a further difficulty in the medieval application of the 2×2 matrix, that it trades upon an ambiguity in 'rational'. In one sense, 'rational' is opposed to 'non-rational' and covers every psychological characteristic that is proper, among animals, to men; but in another, it is opposed to 'irrational', where irrational beliefs and desires may nevertheless be rational in the first sense, but cannot be *justified*, and are therefore false or bad respectively. The desire for respectability is rational in the first sense, but it does not follow that it is rational in the second. Thus chronic conflicts of desires can arise in which bodily appetites play no part. They do, admittedly, engage the emotions, but that is a further ground for suspicion of the 2×2 matrix, which lumps emotions together with bodily appetites in the same compartment.

A chronic conflict of desires may also, and perhaps often does arise

when conscience has been brought into line with the desire for respectability and is then incompatible with the satisfaction of bodily appetites.
Even the medieval writers recognised (correcting Augustine) that
bodily appetites are not bad in themselves, distinguishing the impulse
to sin as a disorder of those appetites (cf. e.g. Aquinas, *Summa theologiae*
3.15.2; 3.27.3). So we also have to allow for chronic conflicts of desires
in which the classical tableau is reversed, conscience being mistaken but
the bodily appetites with which it is at odds being rational in the sense of
justifiable. Here, conscience and the impulse to sin are working in con-
cert against bodily appetite, and the assumption that they are always
necessarily opposed cannot be sustained.

The influence of the predominant medieval account of the impulse to
sin remains so strong, even today, when its origins have long been
forgotten, that we are reluctant to ponder this type of case. In popular
usage, 'immorality' is often synonymous with 'sexual immorality' and,
for all the talk we hear of living today in a 'permissive' society, denying
or severely limiting the satisfaction of sexual appetite remains a substantial component in our notion of a 'respectable citizen'. The rules
enjoined by the desire for respectability may, of course, be independently justifiable, but the concentration upon sexual and other bodily
appetites which it has produced has also deflected attention from aspects
of behaviour which may be more fundamental. Though many would
wish to do so, it is not necessary to reject the doctrine of the impulse to
sin in order to put first things first. The Reformers' doctrine of the total
depravity of fallen human nature was a step in this direction. It has often
been caricatured as asserting that fallen man is totally depraved, but
what they actually meant was that the impulse to sin is not just an
affliction of sensuality which infects reason secondarily; rather, it is
total in the sense of affecting all the psychological powers equally.
Anselm went to the other extreme with his interpretation of the impulse to sin as a corruption of the will, which reverses the rabbinic
account of its effects; instead of being basically a disorder of bodily
appetites which infects reason secondarily through imagination, it becomes basically a disorder of reason which infects bodily appetites
secondarily. Working out the relation of the impulse to sin to conscience will then call for substantial corrections to the medieval view of
the latter: in particular, it could provide an explanation of *why* we are
so unreliable in determining the truth-values of *a priori* deontic propositions, and thus afford a better understanding of mistaken conscience.

Aquinas' treatment of mistaken conscience marks an advance upon

Bonaventure's, because it explicitly introduces the principle that a mistaken conscience excuses *except* where the person concerned ought to have known better. The importance of this principle is not so much that it goes some way towards justifying the modern insistence upon the primacy of conscience, as that it justifies us in saying that people *can* sometimes be caught in a double bind, for there is a great deal of difference between painting oneself into a corner from which there is no escape and being placed there willy-nilly. The account remains incomplete, however, until we have given at least some indication of types of case in which we are justified in saying that a man ought to have known better. One such will be where he had changed his conscience, over a period of time, in such a way that he now believes a deontic proposition which is inconsistent with a true deontic proposition which he used to believe. Unlike Aquinas, however, we should wish to allow that people can be brought up to believe false deontic propositions and may continue to believe them through no fault of their own. A second type of case is when a person misapplies a deontic belief to given circumstances because he describes the circumstances in a certain way, where he can be blamed for his choice of description. These are, above all others, cases in which self-deception is operative. The credit for raising the topic of self-deception in relation to conscience goes to Butler in the eighteenth century, but he greatly underestimated the difficulty in unmasking it, and it may well turn out, when more closely investigated, to provide a link with medieval thought as the strongest evidence for the impulse to sin.

Although, in this survey, I have criticised many of the assumptions, as well as the conclusions of Philip the Chancellor, Bonaventure and Aquinas in their work on conscience, their achievement, taken as a whole, was substantial. Just consider it in relation to the history of European philosophy since Plato: where else can we find such a wide-ranging discussion of the topic, before or since? Moreover, they showed that it is a topic well-deserving of attention from philosophers: important for logic, which has sadly neglected deontic propositions and practical reasoning: raising difficult issues in the philosophy of mind, because it upsets preconceived notions of the inter-relationships between psychological concepts: and effectively sketching out a programme for investigating the foundations of ethics, with the promise of an approach which could link practical philosophy with the developments in theoretical philosophy over the last hundred years. The questions they asked about conscience are only alien to a modern philosopher when taken superficially; when we ponder them, they turn out to have lost little of their relevance and even the distinction between *synderesis* and *conscientia*, in spite of its dubious exegetical origins, led to important results which have not been matched since. To be sure, the outlook of medieval philosophers was limited by the assumptions of the society in which they lived and worked, but it is only retrospectively that we see such limitations at all clearly, and who today can be confident that future generations will not think the same of our philosophical debates? No generation will say the last word on any philosophical topic: Kant's assumption that logic was a closed book, on the eve of its greatest development since Aristotle, stands as a classical warning on that score. On the other hand, many philosophical debates have turned out, in retrospect, to be cul-de-sacs, resting from the start upon assumptions which, once rejected, have made the debate seem largely irrelevant because it stemmed from a misdescription of the problem. The medieval discussion of conscience is not in that category; when its false assumptions have been corrected, the questions do not have to be rejected: at most, some re-formulation is required.

TRANSLATIONS

Notes on the translations

1 *Quotations.* I have translated quotations in the form in which they are given. Medieval writers did not have critical editions of the Bible, the Fathers, etc., at their disposal, with the result that their quotations are often inaccurate. Anyone who looks up the references given should not be surprised, therefore, if the author quoted says something different in that place from what has been attributed to him. Augustine's quotation of Job 28:28 is a good example (cf. Augustine, below, §22). The Revised Standard Version, in general the most accurate among English translations of the Bible, reads:

> Behold, the fear of the Lord, that is wisdom;
> and to depart from evil is understanding.

This does not support Augustine's distinction between wisdom and knowledge. Instead of 'devotion' or 'worship of God' the text has 'the fear of the Lord' and, in any case, the literary form employed is not one of contrast, but of repetition, in which roughly the same thought is expressed twice, in slightly different ways. To have given the RSV translation of Job 28:28 in translating Augustine would thus have made his argument less intelligible and, in general, it is more important, in the present context, to know what a medieval author *thought* his 'authorities' said than what they actually said.

2 *Knowledge.* The medieval vocabulary relating to knowledge does not coincide with ours. The term most frequently used in these texts, '*scientia*', translates the Greek '*episteme*', and normally means an organised body of knowledge rather than a particular piece of knowledge. Unfortunately 'science' has now been pre-empted in English for the natural sciences, which is far narrower than the Latin '*scientia*'. In German, '*Wissenschaft*' is exactly equivalent to the latter. A second term, also used in these texts, but less often, is '*cognitio*'; this is much wider than 'scientia' and even includes perception. Again, there is no ready English equivalent. I have used 'knowledge' to render '*scientia*' and

'apprehension' to render '*cognitio*'. A third and still more problematic term in this group is '*intellectus*', which translates the Greek '*nous*'. Literally, 'thought' is probably the nearest English equivalent, but we do not use 'thought' to mean the ability to think, which is the central notion here, while 'intelligence' is unsuitable, too, because we think of people as being more or less intelligent, whereas no medieval philosopher would have considered men as differing in the amount of *intellectus* with which they could be credited. There is an older, philosophical usage of 'the understanding' which comes close to '*intellectus*', but this is now obsolete and the modern sense of 'understanding' is too narrow. Accordingly, I have judged it best simply to transliterate '*intellectus*' as 'intellect'. Finally, '*ratio*' translates the Greek '*logos*' and has as wide an employment in medieval philosophy as '*logos*' in ancient philosophy. No single translation of '*ratio*' is possible. As a psychological power, it is equivalent to *intellectus* (cf. Aquinas, *Debated Questions on Truth* 15.1) and, in that sense, can be rendered by 'reason'; in other contexts it can mean 'concept', 'definition', and several other things.

3 *The agent intellect and the possible intellect.* These terms derive from Aristotle, *De anima* 3.4–5, where he distinguishes *nous* into an active and a passive potentiality respectively. It is one of the most obscure passages in the whole of Aristotle's writings; from the Greek commentators onwards, the distinction has been variously interpreted. Another book on the pattern of the present one would be necessary to do justice to the topic, so it is better to say no more about it here.

4 *Desire.* The most general term for desire in medieval philosophy is '*appetitus*', which translates the Greek '*orexis*'. Following Plato and Aristotle, rational desire (Greek '*boulesis*', Latin '*voluntas*') is distinguished from non-rational: I have used 'will' to render '*voluntas*'. Non-rational desire is distinguished into *concupiscentia* (Greek '*epithymia*') and *ira* (Greek '*thymos*'). The former comprises all bodily desires and corresponds closely to the older English sense of 'lust', but, as the latter is nowadays restricted to sexual desire, the nearest equivalent is probably 'appetite'. Although 'appetite' means desire for food in the first instance, we do also speak of sexual appetite, though not, perhaps, of an appetite for keeping warm in cold weather or for keeping cool in the heat. '*Ira*' is, literally, 'anger', but includes some other emotions, e.g. fear, as well. I have translated it by 'emotion', although that is probably too wide. This threefold division of desire stems ultimately from Plato's argu-

ment for the tripartite soul in the *Republic* and it is an open question
how far it reflects a philosophical doctrine rather than three kinds of
desire marked linguistically. A conventional translation of the three
Greek/Latin terms is thus virtually unavoidable.

5 *Conscience.* Although '*conscientia*' translates the Greek '*syneidesis*'
(corrupted in medieval texts to '*synderesis*'?), it cannot be rendered here
by 'conscience', because the medieval writers wish to distinguish between *synderesis* and *conscientia*. The etymological connection between '*conscientia*' and '*scientia*' is also important both to Bonaventure
(1.1) and to Aquinas (17.1). It would, in general, give a totally false
impression of the medieval account of conscience to translate either of
these terms by 'conscience'. Yet the distinctions which they wish to
draw are not marked in English (any more than in Latin or in Greek),
so there is no alternative but to leave them untranslated. (On one or
two occasions it has been possible to render '*conscientia*' as 'conscience'
without misleading.) This makes the translations less easy to read, but
that seemed preferable to imposing a misleading interpretation upon
them.

6 Synderesis *as a natural tribunal.* The latin '*naturale iudicatorium*' translates Basil the Great's phrase '*kriterion physikon*', 'since we have within
us a certain natural tribunal, by which we tell good from bad' (*Homily
on the Beginning of the Book of Proverbs*, §9; Migne, *Patrologia Graeca*,
vol. 31, col. 405C). Bonaventure uses this phrase in a citation from
Augustine, *On Free Choice* 3.20, where Augustine himself says '*naturale
iudicium*': 'It is enough to receive, before every desert for a good deed,
a natural judgement by which wisdom is preferred to error ...' It
crops up again in Aquinas, who attributes the 'rules of and insights into
(*lumina*) the virtues' which, according to Augustine, are 'true and unchangeable and ... are there to be contemplated by those who have the
strength to gaze on them, each with his own reason and mind' (*ibid.*
2.10) to 'the natural tribunal which we call "*synderesis*"', although
Augustine merely describes them as 'rules of wisdom'.

7 *The impulse to sin.* I have used this phrase to translate '*fomes*', the
origin and meaning of which is discussed above, pp. 22–25. *Fomes* was
not always distinguished from *concupiscentia*. Thus, to cite an early and a
late example, Peter Lombard uses the terms interchangeably, while one

of the canons of the Council of Trent states: 'This holy synod acknow-
ledges and declares that *concupiscentia* or *fomes* remains even in the baptised; . . . The holy synod proclaims that the Catholic Church has never
understood this *concupiscentia*, which the Apostle sometimes calls "sin"
(Romans 6:12 ff), to be called "sin" because it is truly and properly sin
in the reborn, but because it derives from sin and turns us towards sin.
But if anyone declares the contrary, let him be anathema' (Session v,
Decree on Original Sin 5 (1546)).

8 '*General*'. I have used 'general' throughout to translate '*universalis*'.
'Universal' would suggest, to a modern reader, 'universally quantified',
whereas an existentially quantified proposition is as much a generalisation as a universally quantified one. (Wherever the logical structure of a
proposition can be represented with the aid of one of the two quantifiers, it can also be represented with the aid of the other, together with
negation; nor, if we are concerned with the meaning of the proposition,
is it always possible to say whether a proposition is negative or affirmative.) Moreover, Aquinas cites some examples of general propositions
which are not universally quantified, so 'general' would appear the
safer translation.

Jerome (c. 347–419)

Born in north-east Yugoslavia to wealthy Christian parents, Jerome was sent to Rome when about 12 for his education, in the course of which he became addicted to the Greek and Latin classics and learned to write extremely good Latin. After a strenuous social life, he was baptised about 365 and decided, to the disappointment of his family, to become a monk. About 374 he joined the hermits in the Syrian desert behind Antioch, taking the opportunity to learn Hebrew. In 382 he returned to Rome to become secretary to Pope Damasus and played a central part in the campaign for imposing celibacy upon priests. The next pope did not much like him, so he returned to the east with two Roman ladies and founded a monastery in Bethlehem, where he devoted the rest of his life to scholarship. He is best known for his Latin translation of the Bible, the Vulgate, but in his day was a great satirist and controversialist, which made him many enemies.

COMMENTARY ON EZEKIEL, 1.7

(Latin text in Migne, *Patrologia Latina*, vol. 25, col. 22)

Most people interpret the man, the lion and the ox as the rational, emotional and appetitive parts of the soul, following Plato's division, who calls them the *logikon* and *thymikon* and *epithymetikon*, locating reason in the brain, emotion in the gall-bladder and appetite in the liver. And they posit a fourth part which is above and beyond these three, and which the Greeks call *synteresin*: that spark of conscience which was not even extinguished in the breast of Cain after he was turned out of Paradise, and by which we discern that we sin, when we are overcome by pleasures or frenzy and meanwhile are misled by an imitation of reason. They reckon that this is, strictly speaking, the eagle, which is not mixed up with the other three, but corrects them when they go wrong, and of which we read in Scripture as the spirit 'which intercedes for us with ineffable groaning' (Romans 8:26). 'For no one knows what a man is really like, except the spirit which is in him' (1 Corinthians 2:11). And, writing to the Thessalonians, Paul also entreats for it to be kept sound together with soul and body (1 Thessalonians 5:23). However, we also see that this conscience is cast down in some people, who have neither shame nor insight regarding their offences, and loses its place, as is written in the book of Proverbs: 'When the wicked man reaches the depths of sin, he doesn't care a damn.' (Proverbs 18:3.) So they deserve to be told: 'You have acquired the face of a prostitute, you refuse to blush' (Jeremiah 3:3),

Augustine (354–430)

Born in Souk Ahras, eastern Algeria, to a Christian mother and pagan father. Educated in the pagan schools of north Africa, he became fond of Latin literature but found Greek difficult. After twelve years as a teacher in Souk Ahras, during which he became a Manichean, he went to Rome in 383 and was appointed to the chair of Rhetoric at Milan, where he came under the influence of Ambrose. After a mystical experience, he became a Christian in 387, returned to Souk Ahras in 388 and founded a monastery. He was ordained priest in 391, became auxiliary bishop of Hippo, near Tunis, four years later, and bishop of Hippo in 396. His voluminous writings were enormously influential throughout the middle ages; he engaged in many local controversies, but is best known for his autobiography, the Confessions. *In addition to some biblical commentaries, he wrote two major works,* The City of God *and* On the Trinity. *The passage from the latter translated below expounds his distinction between wisdom and knowledge, which is referred to by Philip the Chancellor, Bonaventure and Aquinas as the distinction between higher and lower reason in their treatises on conscience. At the end, there is an interpretation of the dialogue between Socrates and the slave-boy in Plato's* Meno, *which is taken up by Bonaventure.*

ON THE TRINITY, BOOK 12 (excerpts)

(Latin text in *Sancti Aurelii Augustini, De Trinitate libri XV*. Turnholt: Brepols, 1968. *Corpus Christianorum, series Latina*, vol. 50, pp. 356–379).

2 Animals other than man can also perceive external bodies by their bodily senses and, having fixed them in memory, remember them, and strive after those which are expedient, shun those which are disagreeable. But to observe them: to retain them not only when they are grasped naturally but also when they are purposely committed to memory: to impress them again by recalling and thinking about them at the moment they are falling into oblivion so that, just as thought is formed from what is carried in memory, what is in memory may be strengthened by thought; to construct fictitious sights by taking no

matter what of what is recalled from one occasion and from another and, as it were, sewing it together: to examine how what is specious in this area, not in spiritual but in bodily matters, may be distinguished from what is true – these and like actions, although done in respect of what is perceptible and what the mind has derived thence through bodily sense, are neither done without the participation of reason nor common to men and other animals. But it belongs to higher reason (*ratio sublimior*) to judge these bodily things by incorporeal and ever-lasting criteria which, if they were not above the human mind, would not really be unchangeable; yet, if something of us were not sub-ordinately united to them, we could not judge bodily things by them. Moreover, we judge bodily things by criteria of size and shape, which the mind knows to persist unchangeably.

3 That in us which is thus engaged in dealing with bodily and temporal actions, since it is not common to us and the other animals, is certainly rational, but drawn, as it were, from that rational substance of our mind by which we hang on, from below, to intelligible and unchangeable truth and is calculated to treat of and govern lower things. For just as there was not found among all the animals a helpmate for man who was like him, apart from there being taken out of him one formed to be his wife, so too there is no comparable help for [that part of] our mind by which we reflect upon higher and internal truth from the parts of the soul which we have in common with other animals in that use of bodily things which is adequate to human nature. Hence something rational in us is apportioned to have this function as its work, not separated so as to sever unity, but as if diverted to aid partnership. And just as there are two in one flesh in male and female, so the one nature of mind embraces both our understanding and action, or deliberation and execution, or reason and rational desire, or anything by which they can otherwise be more significantly expressed. Thus, as it was said of the former, 'They shall be two in one flesh' (Genesis 2:24; Matthew 19:5; 1 Corinthians 6:16; Ephesians 5:31), it can be said of the latter: 'Two in one mind'.

10 But it is to be observed why what the apostle says, that not woman but man (*vir*) is the image of God (1 Corinthians 11.7) is not contradict-ory to what is written in Genesis: 'God made man (*homo*) in the image of God; he made him male and female; he made them and he blessed them' (1:27–28; 5:1–2; cf. 9:6). The latter says that human nature itself,

which is complete in both sexes, was made 'in the image of God', nor does it separate females from what is to be understood as the image of God. For having said that 'God made man (*homo*) in the image of God', it continues 'he made him male and female' or, on another reading, 'he made them male and female', at any rate. How then do we hear from the apostle that man (*vir*) is the image of God and so is forbidden to cover his head, whereas woman is not and is therefore ordered to do so? Only, I believe, in virtue of what I was just saying when I discussed the nature of the human mind: that a woman together with her husband is the image of God, so that that whole substance is one image. But when she is considered as [man's] helper, that which belongs to her alone is not the image of God, whereas that which belongs to man (*vir*) alone is the image of God as fully and integrally as when she is joined into unity with it. As we said about the nature of the human mind, it is the image of God when, as a whole, it contemplates truth and is still, to the extent that it deliberates about truth which has been seen, the image of God when something is apportioned from it and diverted for a given purpose to action respecting temporal things, but not the image of God to the extent that it is aimed at lower deeds. And, because it is the more conformed to the image of God the more it strives after what is eternal and thus ought not to be restrained so that it is confined and restrained from [the eternal], 'a man ought not to cover his head'. But, because too great an advance towards lower things is dangerous to that rational action which is directed towards bodily and temporal things, there ought to be some power exercised over its head, which is proclaimed by the covering by which it is signified to be restrained.

12 For man is made in the image of God not in the form of his body but in his rational mind, as not only the most truthful reason but also the authority of the apostle himself makes clear. It is indeed an ugly and vain thought which holds God to be delimited and defined by the features of bodily members. Moreover, does not the same blessed apostle say: 'Be renewed in the spirit of your mind and put on the new man, [put on] him who is created in accordance with God' (Ephesians 4:23–24)? And elsewhere, he says more explicitly: 'Putting off the old man with his deeds, put on the new one who is renewed by recognition of God through the image of him who created him' (Colossians 3:9–10). If, then, we are renewed in the spirit of our mind, and he 'who is renewed by recognition of God, through the image of him who created him' is the new man, there can be no doubt that man is made in the

image of him who created him neither in the body nor in just any part of the soul, but in the rational mind, where there can be recognition of God. But it is by this renewal that we are also made sons of God through Christian baptism and, putting on the new man, we put on Christ, in particular, by faith (cf. Galatians 3 :26–27). Who, then, would deprive women of this partnership, since they are co-heirs of grace with us? And the same apostle says in another passage: 'You are all sons of God through faith in Jesus Christ. For every one of you who has been baptised in Christ has put on Christ. There is neither Jew nor Greek, neither slave nor free man, neither male nor female: all of you are one in Christ Jesus' (Galatians 3 :26–28). Surely the female faithful have not lost the sex of their bodies? Rather, they are there renewed in the image of God, where there is no sex, and because man is there made in the image of God, where there is no sex, i.e. in the spirit of his mind. Why, then, is a man on that account not obliged to cover his head, because he is the image and glory of God, but a woman is [so] obliged, because she is the glory of man – as though a woman were not renewed in the spirit of her mind, which is renewed in recognition of God in accordance with the image of him who created him? Because, since she differs in bodily sex from a man, her bodily covering could represent that the part of reason which is diverted to regulate temporal matters does not remain the image of God except to the extent that the human mind (which it is clear that not only males but also females have) clings to seeing and deliberating about eternal notions. [13] In their minds, there-fore, a common nature is discerned, but in their bodies an apportion-ment of that one mind is represented.

Having climbed within, by certain steps of examination, through the parts of the soul, [we find that] reason, in which the inner man can be recognised, starts at the point where something begins to happen which is not common to us and the other animals. If [the inner man] should also slide too far in an uncontrolled progress towards externals, through that reason to which the administration of temporal matters is dele-gated, his head consenting to it (I mean that what presides as the male part in the watch-tower of deliberation does not restrain or bridle [that progress]), then he will have 'begun to grow old among his enemies' (Psalm 6:8), viz. the demons with their prince the devil, envious of virtue. And the sight of eternal things is withdrawn from the head, itself, too, for eating forbidden [fruit] with its wife, so that 'the light of its eyes is no longer with it' (Psalm 37:11) ... [14] ... and so, allured by bodily forms and changes, because it does not have them within it, it is enveloped by their images, which it fixes in memory, and is foully polluted by fantasy-fornication, turning all its energies to those ends by which it inquisitively seeks bodily and temporal things through the bodily senses, either aspiring, with swollen arrogance, to be higher than other souls given over to the bodily senses, or plunging into a muddy swirl of bodily pleasure.

17 Let us now complete . . . the discussion which we began about the part of reason to which knowledge (*scientia*) belongs, that is, the apprehension (*cognitio*) of temporal and changeable things necessary for the conduct of this life. For, just as, in that literal marriage of the two people who were made first, the serpent did not eat from the forbidden tree but merely persuaded [them] to eat, and the woman did not eat alone but gave [the fruit] to her man and they ate together, although she alone spoke with the serpent and she alone was led astray by him (cf. Genesis 3:1–6), so too, in that hidden and secret marriage which is also displayed and discerned in one man, the bodily or, as I may say, the sensory movement of the soul which is directed to the bodily senses, is shut out from the reckoning of wisdom (*sapientia*). Bodily things are indeed perceived by the bodily senses; eternal and unchangeable things are understood by virtue of wisdom. But desire is near to the reckonings of knowledge, since what is called the knowledge of actions reasons about those bodily things which are perceived by the bodily senses: if well, so that it may relate its observations to the highest good as its end: if badly, however, so that it may enjoy them as good things such that it may completely rest in them in false happiness. Whenever, therefore, that bodily or animal sense obtrudes some enticement to enjoy itself upon that application of the mind which is directed towards temporal and bodily things because of its job of reasoning tenaciously about action – [to enjoy itself], that is, as if with a private and exclusive good and not as if with a public and common good which is unchangeable – it is like the serpent speaking to the woman. So to consent to this enticement is to eat of the forbidden tree.

19 This argument, then – by which we have sought in the mind of each man a kind of conceptual marriage of contemplation and action, with roles assigned separately to each yet preserving the unity of the mind in both, and holding to the truth of that narrative which divine authority hands down concerning the first two human beings, viz. the man

and his woman from which the human race was propagated – is only to be accepted in so far as the apostle may be understood, by assigning the image of God only to the man and not also to the woman, to have meant something in the different sexes of the two people which may be sought in a single person.

21 But whether the apostle's saying that man is the image and glory of God but woman the glory of man is to be taken in this or that sense or in some other way, it is clear that when we live in accord with God, our mind, directed towards his invisible things, ought progressively to be formed by his eternity, truth and love, yet that something of our rational effort, i.e. of the same kind, should be directed to the use of changeable and bodily things, without which this life cannot be carried on: not that it should be conformed to 'this age' (cf. Romans 12:2) by making such good things its end and by twisting the desire for happiness towards them, but so that whatever we do rationally in our use of temporal things, we may do through contemplation of those eternal things which are to be attained, passing through the former, cleaving to the latter. For knowledge also has its own good measure if that in it which puffs up or tends to puff up is overcome by love of eternal things, which does not puff up but, as we know, builds up (cf. 1 Corinthians 8:1). Indeed, without knowledge the very virtues, by which one lives correctly and by which this unhappy life is so regulated that it may attain to that eternal one which is truly happy, cannot be had.

22 Yet the action by which we use temporal things well differs from the contemplation of eternal things, and the latter is reckoned to wisdom, the former to knowledge ... I find it written in the book of Job, where that holy man is himself speaking: 'See, devotion (*pietas*) is wisdom, but to keep away from evil things is knowledge' (28:28). In this distinction, contemplation is to be understood to belong to wisdom, action to knowledge. For by 'devotion' here, he meant 'worship of God', which in Greek is called '*theosebeia*', since this sentence contains that word in the Greek manuscripts. And what is there more excellent among eternal things than God, whose nature alone is unchangeable? And what else is worship of him but love of him, by which we desire now to see him and believe and hope that we shall see him and, to the extent that we make progress, 'see now through a mirror, in a riddle, but then "with clarity"'? For that is what the apostle Paul says, 'face to face' (1 Corinthians 13:12) ... Talk about these and similar things

seems to me to be talk of wisdom. 'But to keep away from evil things',
which Job says to be knowledge, is without any doubt about temporal
things, because it is through time that we are among evil things, from
which we ought to hold aloof so that we may come to those eternal
good things. For this reason, whatever we do wisely, bravely, temper-
ately and justly, belongs to that knowledge or training by which our
action is directed towards avoiding evil and desiring good, together
with whatever we accumulate from knowledge (*cognitio*) of historical
lessons, by way of examples to be avoided or imitated and by way of
everything which is suited to our necessary purposes.

23 When we talk of these things, I consider it to be talk of knowledge,
to be distinguished from talk of wisdom, which is concerned with what
neither was nor will be but is and, in virtue of that eternity in which it
is, is said to have been and to be and to be going to be without any
temporal variation. For [these things] did not exist in such a way that
they should cease to exist, nor are they going to exist as though they do
not exist now, but always had and always will have had the same existence. They do not persist, however, as though fixed in spatial locations
like bodies, but are present to a mental glance as intelligible in their
incorporeal nature, just as the former visible or tangible things in space
are to the bodily senses. But not only do intelligible and incorporeal
concepts (*ratio*) of perceptible things which occupy places persist without spatial locations; there are also intelligible, rather than perceptible,
[concepts] of changes over time, without temporal passage. To reach
these by sharpness (*acies*) of mind is given to few and, when they are
reached so far as is possible, the man who reaches them does not himself
remain in them, but is repulsed like the front line of an army (*acies*)
beaten back, and a passing thought occurs of something which is not
transitory. Yet this passing thought is committed to memory through
the training by which the soul has been instructed, so that, though
forced to pass on, it may be able to return. If, however, thought should
not return to memory and find there what it had committed to it, it
would be led to [the concept] like an ignorant person, as it was led
before, and would find it where it had originally found it, in that
incorporeal truth, from which it may be fixed again in memory, as
though written down. For it is not as the incorporeal and unchangeable
concept persists in, for example, a square body that a man's thought
persists in [the concept], if indeed it can reach it at all without imagining
a spatial location. Or again, if one were to grasp, timelessly in a hidden

and deep silence, the rhythm of an artistic and musical sound extending over a period of time, it could at least be thought of so long as that melody could be heard. Yet what even a passing mental glance will have been able to snatch from it and will have stored up in memory (like swallowing into the stomach), one will be able, by remembering, to chew over and to translate what one has thereby learned into systematic knowledge (*disciplina*). But if it should have been wholly erased by forgetfulness, then, led by teaching, one will come again to what he had altogether lost and so it will be found just as it was.

24 Thus the famous philosopher Plato tried to persuade us that the souls of men lived before they bore these bodies, and hence that what is learned is something apprehended which is remembered, rather than something newly apprehended. For he asked us to consider that some boy or other, questioned about geometry, replied as though he were most expert in that discipline: questioned step by step and ingeniously, he saw what was to be seen and said what he saw [cf. *Meno* 80D–86C]. But if this were recollection of things previously apprehended, not everyone, at any rate, or not quite everyone, could do this when questioned in this way, because not all were geometers in the earlier life, since the latter are so rare among the human race that it is hardly possible to find any. But one should believe, rather, that the nature of the intelligent mind is so constructed as to see, by a certain incorporeal light which is *sui generis*, what is subsumed to intelligible things through arrangement by their author in a natural ordering: just as the eye of flesh sees what is near to and around it in this bodily light, of which light it is receptive and to which it corresponds. For neither does this [eye] distinguish white from black without a teacher because it was already acquainted with them before it was created in this flesh. Finally, why is it only with respect to intelligible things that everyone who is questioned well should reply with what pertains to each discipline although ignorant of the latter? Why can no one do this with respect to perceptible things, except for those which he has seen while established in the body or believed when those acquainted with them pointed them out, either in writing or verbally? . . .

25 If, therefore, the correct distinction between wisdom and knowledge is that wisdom is concerned with the intellectual apprehension of eternal things but knowledge with rational apprehension of temporal things, it is not difficult to judge which should be put before or put

after which. But if some other distinction ought to be held by which the difference between these two ought to be known – which without any doubt the apostle teaches to be distinct, saying: 'To some, indeed, the discussion of wisdom is given by the spirit, to others the discussion of knowledge by the same spirit' (1 Corinthians 12:8) – still, the clearest distinction between the two things which we have posited is that the intellectual apprehension of eternal things is one thing, rational [apprehension] of temporal things another, and that no one doubts that the former is to be preferred to the latter.

Peter Lombard (died about 1160)

Peter was born near Novara, educated at Bologna, Rheims and the school of St Victor, and was probably also a pupil of Abelard. He taught in the cathedral school of Paris from 1140 until he became bishop of Paris in 1159. He wrote the first theological text-book, called the Sententiae *(Judgements), published in the early 1150s. It consisted of a series of questions on which arguments on both sides were given from Scripture, the Councils and the Fathers (taken from earlier anthologies), and then, usually, his own judgement on the issue. The* Sententiae *quickly became established as the standard theology text, after the Bible, in the new universities, and over two hundred commentaries were written upon it. The question translated below, though concerned with the will rather than conscience, contains a reference to the passage from Jerome's* Commentary on Ezekiel *translated above, and thus became the source of the medieval treatises on conscience; most of them are commentaries upon this question.*

BOOKS OF JUDGEMENTS 2.39

(Latin text in *Magistri Petri Lombardi Sententiae in IV libros distinctae*, tom. I, pars II. Grottaferrata (Rome), *Collegium S. Bonaventurae Ad Claras Aquas* (Quaracchi), 1971, pp. 553–556.)

Chapter 1 (249)

1 *Since will is one of those things which man has naturally, why it is said to sin, when nothing else which is natural is sinful.* A pretty necessary question arises here, by reason of what was discussed previously. For it was said above that will is naturally present in man, just as thought and memory are. But whatever is natural to man does not prevail over a goodness which God will hardly allow it to exhaust. For example, thought or reason, and abilities and memory, even though they be clouded over and corrupted, are nevertheless good and are not called sins, as Augustine clearly shows: 'This is', he says, 'the image in which men are

created, by which they are set over the other animals. And this creature, the most excellent among created things, is changed from a deformed form to a well-formed form when it is justified by God. For there were also good natures among defects' (*On the Trinity* 15.8). But this image is reason or thought. Hence, since will is among natural things, why is it not always good, even though it is sometimes subject to defects?

2 *An answer which some people give.* To this, those answer superficially who say that everything which is, in so far as it is, is good: because they maintain that the will in so far as it is, or in so far as it is the will, is good, as we said above (35.2), but that, to the extent that it is disordered, is bad and sinful.

3 For, in that case, we can reasonably ask these people: If the will, to the extent that it is disordered, is sinful, why then are not thought, reason and abilities and so on, sinful when they are disordered? For they are indeed disordered just like the will when they are not directed to a right goal and are exercised in collusion with it. – To which they reply that by the noun 'will' is sometimes signified a power, viz. the natural potentiality of willing, and sometimes the exercise of this power. The power itself, naturally innate to the soul, is never sinful, just like the power of remembering or of thinking; but the exercise of this power, which is also called 'will', is sinful whenever it is disordered.

Chapter 2 (250)

1 *Why an exercise of the will may be a sin, though exercises of other potentialities are not sins.* But it is asked, further, why an exercise of this natural potentiality may be a sin, although exercises of other potentialities, e.g. of the potentiality of memory, whose exercise consists in remembering, and of the potentiality of thought, whose exercise consists in thinking, are not.

Reply: To this, the same people say: because the exercise of will is of a different kind from the exercise of memory or thought. The former is exercised in order to obtain something or not to allow it, which cannot be done in regard to what is bad without it itself being bad. For it is bad to want what is bad, but is not bad to think about or remember what is bad. – *That even exercises of memory and of thought are sometimes said to be bad.* Although some of them not incorrectly maintain that even these exercises are occasionally bad. For now and again a person remembers something bad in order to do it, and seeks to understand the truth in order to attack it. – This, then, is how the question put forward is resolved by those who hold everything to be good in so far as it is.

2 *Another answer.* Those who actually say that bad wills are sins and in no way good answer more briefly, saying that exercise of the will is not something natural, but only the power and potentiality of willing, which is always good, and in everyone, even in children in whom there is not yet any exercise of it.

Chapter 3 (251)

1 *How the following is to be understood: A man, even one who is a slave to sin, naturally wants what is good.* It should further be asked how we are to understand what Ambrose says, expounding the apostle's saying: 'For I do not do what I want, but do what I do not want.' For he says that 'man, subject to sin, does what he does not want, because he naturally wants what is good, but this will always lack in effect, unless the grace of God helps and frees it' (Ambrosiaster, *Commentary on Romans* 7:15,18). If man is subject to sin, he indeed wants and works evil, because he is a slave to sin, and his will, as Augustine says (*Enchiridion* 30), acts freely. How, then, can it naturally want what is good?

2 *Does a man naturally want what is good and freely serve sin by the same will, or not?* Is it the same will, that is, the same motivation by which he freely serves sin and by which he naturally wants what is good? If it is not the same will, which of these, therefore, is it which, when a man is justified, is delivered from slavery to sin? As we have argued above (26.1), the grace of God frees and helps man's will, which he prepares by helping it and helps once prepared. But what is this will? That which naturally wants what is good, or that which freely serves sin, if there are really two wills?

3 *The question proposed is followed up first by those who say that these are two sources of change.* A deep question has been raised, which different people determine by expounding it in various ways. For some say that there are two motivations, one by which a man naturally wants what is good. Why naturally? And why is it called 'natural'? Because such was the motivation of human nature in its original state, in which we were

created without any defect, and this is properly called 'nature'. For man was created with a righteous will. Thus it is written in *On Church teachings*: 'It is to be held most firmly that the first men were created good and righteous, with free choice, by which they could, if they wanted, sin by their own will; and they sinned not from necessity, but by their own will.' (Fulgentius, *To Peter, on Faith* 25). Man is therefore rightly said naturally to want what is good, because he was constructed with a good and righteous will. For the higher spark of reason which, as Jerome says, could not even be extinguished in Cain, always wants what is good and hates what is bad (*Commentary on Ezekiel* 1.7). Others, however, say that there is a mental motivation by which the mind, having abandoned the law of higher things, subjects itself to sins and is attracted by them. Before grace is present to someone, this motivation, according to them, tyrannises and rules over man and suppresses the other motivation. However, this is by free choice. When grace comes, the bad motivation is crushed and the other, naturally good one is freed and helped so that it is effective in wanting what is good. But before grace, although a man naturally wants what is good, yet it must not be allowed without qualification that he has a good will, but rather an evil one.

4 *According to others, there is said to be only one will.* Others, however, say that there is one will, that is one motivation, by which a man naturally wants what is good and through a defect in it wants and takes pleasure in what is evil; so that, to the extent that it wants what is good, it is naturally good but, to the extent that it wants what is bad, it is evil.

Philip the Chancellor (died 1236)

Almost nothing is known about the life of Philip the Chancellor. His title indicates that he was chancellor of the diocese of Paris. His work Summa de bono, *written about 1230, has still not been printed, apart from some questions on the soul from the first part and the treatise on conscience translated here. It was, however, widely influential for about a century.*

SUMMA DE BONO, Treatise on Conscience

(Latin text in O. Lottin, *Psychologie et morale aux XIIe et XIIIe siècles*, vol. 2. Gembloux, J. Duculot, 1948, pp. 140–142, 145–148, 150–152, 153–156; I have added the headings.)

About *synderesis*, which is called the spark of conscience, which was never extinguished in Cain, and whose job is to murmur back in answer to sin and to correct mistakes, as is said in Jerome's *Commentary on Ezekiel*, we now have to enquire:

1 is it a potentiality of the soul or some connatural disposition which is in the soul from the beginning?

2 if it is a potentiality, is it the higher or the lower part of reason, as Augustine divides the latter in *On the Trinity* and Peter Lombard repeats in the *Judgements*?

3 if there exists the power of sinning in respect of it, as in respect of free choice, whence has this arisen?

4 in what sense is it extinguished and in what sense not, and in respect of what?

1 *Is* synderesis *a potentiality of the soul or an innate disposition?*

A *Arguments that it is a potentiality:*

1 That it is a potentiality of the soul may be supposed from what blessed Gregory [actually, Jerome] says on the text of Ezekiel 1, 'and the four had the face of an eagle at the back', for he says: 'Most people interpret the man, the lion and the ox as rationality and emotion and appetite, following Plato's distinction, who calls them the *logicon* and *thymicon* and *epithymicon*, locating reason in the brain, emotion in the gall-bladder and instinct in the liver. They posit a fourth which is above and beyond these, which the Greeks call *synderesis*: the spark of *conscientia* which, also, was not extinguished in Cain.' Therefore, since what is classified with potentialities will be a potentiality, *synderesis* will be a potentiality or power of the soul, since the rest are powers of the soul.

2 That it is a potentiality of the soul may, moreover, be supposed from what is said at the end of Malachi 2, for Jerome says of the text 'protect your spirit and the wife of your youth' (Malachi 2.15) that the wife of one's youth is the natural law written in our hearts which is wedded to our spirit; it says 'the spirit', not the flesh, which is not pleasing to God: not the animal part, which does not perceive the things which are of God, but the rational spirit which intercedes for us with ineffable groanings, as is said to the Romans (Romans 8.26). But it is established that this spirit is a power of the soul having a view of and a desire for God. Therefore, since this spirit is no other than *synderesis, synderesis* will be a power of the soul.

3 'Now we have received not the spirit of the world, but the spirit which is from God, that we might understand the gifts bestowed on us by God' (1 Corinthians 2:12). Commentary: 'this is not that spirit of ours by which we exist, because it is one thing that we receive in order that we should exist and another which we receive in order that we should be holy. In Scripture, "the spirit of man" means the soul itself or the rational potentiality of the soul. For he gave us a nature in order that we may exist, a soul in order that we may live, a mind in order that we may think.' [Anselm of Laon.]

4 That it is a power of the soul may also be supposed on purely rational grounds:

(a) Since there is a power of the soul which contemplates the truth, which is always being exercised and which philosophers call 'the active intellect' ('intelligence' by Master Richard of St Victor, and similarly by Boethius in his book *On the Consolations of Philosophy*), in the same way there will be another which is disposed to what is good and loathes what is evil, and this is *synderesis*; hence *synderesis* will be a power of the soul.

(b) Sensuality and *synderesis* are said to be contrary with respect to their tendencies, in that just as sensuality inclines reason to follow after what is contingently good and to shun evils contrary to this, so *synderesis* inclines reason to what is good without qualification and draws reason or free choice back from what is bad without qualification. Therefore, since sensuality is a motive power of the soul from its lower part, there will be another power which, to the extent that it works of itself, tends towards what is good without qualification, and this is *synderesis*.

(c) John of Damascus distinguishes the will into a will which is called 'natural' and a deliberating will (*On the Orthodox Faith* 36.11). But it is established that *synderesis* is not a deliberating will, for it is not this which always murmurs back in reply to sin and which corrects mistakes; rather, it is in accordance with this that sin is committed and reason goes wrong, so it will not be that. Hence there will be a natural will which only desires what is good and which is innate to the rational soul, as he says there. Therefore, since the one is a power of the soul, the other will be a power of the soul.

B Arguments that it is a disposition:

It is, however, also argued that it is a disposition, as follows:

1 *Proheresis* [*proairesis*, preferential choice] rightly seems to be contrary to *synderesis*, just as natural is to deliberating will. Thus, as *proheresis* is a disposition by which the deliberating will, an existing power of the soul, is regulated, so too *synderesis* is a disposition arising naturally in conjunction with that potentiality by which the natural will is directed to what is good without qualification.

2 Since the soul is not abandoned by its creator so that it has no help in

doing what is good, just as it contains an impulse to sin inclining free choice towards sin or evil, so, therefore, there will be some aid which, to the extent that it works of itself, always directs it towards what is good and makes it shun what is bad, in the same way as the impulse to sin is related to it contrariwise. But what else can this be except *synderesis*? Therefore *synderesis* will be an aid outside the substance of the soul just as the impulse [to sin] is not of the substance of the soul.

3 Just as there is a certain light in perception, separate from the receptive perceptory potentiality, so there is also in thought, separate from the thinking potentiality, and in desire, separate from the motivating potentiality. Therefore, since *synderesis* is what occupies the place of the light which sets desire aflame, *synderesis* will not be a power but a disposition.

Discussion:

Synderesis, although the morphology of its name makes it sound more like a disposition than a potentiality, is nevertheless the name of a dispositional potentiality: I do not say of an acquired disposition, but of an innate one. And thus, *qua* disposition it can be applied to what is related to it as a disposition, *qua* potentiality to what is related to it as a potentiality. From this it follows that it has a certain opposition to free choice, a certain opposition to the impulse [to sin] and sensuality, and a certain opposition to *proheresis*, which is part of free choice: *qua* potentiality, it is disparate from free choice and from sensuality, *qua* disposition it is disparate from *proheresis* and the impulse [to sin].

So, if anyone asks whether it is a potentiality or a disposition, the right answer lies in taking something in between: a dispositional potentiality. From this, it can be seen in what sense the arguments on both sides are true. The authorities Ezekiel 1, Malachi 2 and 1 Corinthians 2 show that it is a potentiality but from *proheresis* and the impulse [to sin] it is also shown that it is a disposition. And we say that it is in between, a dispositional potentiality.

If, too, anyone asks whether it is natural will, of which John of Damascus speaks, or falls under it, it should be said that the natural will of which he speaks embraces many things, as he himself says, because it is concerned with good things which are rational, and those which are natural, and those which are life-giving, whereas *synderesis* is concerned only with good things which are rational.

To the objection that *synderesis* must be a disposition separate from

the substance of the soul, like light from the power of perception, it is
to be said that this is not so: it is related to reason as an intrinsic light,
because together with the potentiality it makes one and the same thing.

2 *Is* synderesis *the same as free choice or as reason?*

Thus, if it is a power of the soul, we have to ask whether it is the same as
free choice or as reason, or not the same.

A Arguments that it is not the same:

1 From what Gregory says in his commentary on Ezekiel 1 cited
above. For he says that we posit a fourth part of the soul, which the
Greeks call *synderesis*, which is beyond and above these, not mixed up
with the three but correcting their mistakes. Therefore, since one of
them is reason, *synderesis* will be outside the scope of reason, not being
blended with it.

2 Reason is divided into two portions, as Augustine says, one of which
is suited to men but the other, which has to be fed and is called the
lower part of reason, to women. Both of these sin, the latter by seeking
pleasure (*delectatio*), the former by consent. *Synderesis*, however, as such
always murmurs back in answer to sin. Therefore it is neither part of
reason; therefore it must be a distinct power from reason.

B Arguments that it is the same:

1 What is said at the end of 1 Thessalonians on the text 'your spirit
together with soul and body' etc. (5.23) seems to go against the above,
because the interlinear commentary says that 'spirit' is to be understood
as reason. But spirit is there taken to be *synderesis* as Gregory has it in his
commentary on Ezekiel 1: for he says that this is the spirit which intercedes for us with ineffable groanings . . . hence Paul says 'your spirit
together with soul and body'. The commentary on the latter passage,
'your spirit and soul', gives a cross-reference to Ephesians 4:23, 'be renewed in the spirit of your minds'. What is the mind which serves the
law of God? 'It is to be kept sound', that is, 'our reason is to be kept
sound, not consenting to the flesh' etc. And the commentary says:
'Note that he lays down three things as constituting a man: spirit, soul,
body: i.e. that by which we think and that by which we live and that by
which we are visible and tangible, two of which are mentioned again,

because the soul is often cited together with the spirit.' But *synderesis* is not that by which we live or by which we are visible. Therefore it is that by which we think.

2 Letter to the Hebrews 4: 'the word of God is living', etc., 'piercing to the division of soul and spirit'. The ordinary commentary: 'because a son of God learns how sensuality is divided from reason, and the latter from itself when, devoted more to the lowest things it is lower, or more worthy when drawn back from them. Thus we also see how the spirit is divided from itself, when it either stands in awe at the thought of the divine being, or at a lower level ponders heavenly things, or at a yet lower level investigates what it is right to do in worldly matters on earth, or even, how the spirit, that is, reason, is set aside by sensuality, when what is lower in it, i.e. in reason, overcomes what is higher in it.'

3 The commentary on many occasions supposes three motivational powers, as in the parable in Matthew 13:33, 'The kingdom of heaven is like leaven which a woman took and hid in three measures of flour.' The commentary: 'just as spirit, soul and body are not out of harmony with each other, or like the three powers of the soul are drawn together for a single purpose, e.g. we possess practical wisdom (*prudentia*) in our reason, hatred of vice in emotion [*ira*, lit. 'anger'] and a longing for virtue in appetite [*cupiditas*, lit. 'lust']'. But since, according to Augustine, there are no further motivations, and *synderesis* is neither of the latter, it is therefore rational.

4 Gregory says, commenting on Job 'I alone have escaped to tell you' (Job 1:15,16,19), 'one escaped: that is, whatever reason – which has been caught by a sudden onset – calculates that it has lost, it may recover when bowed down with heartfelt contrition' (Gregory the Great, *Morals on the Book of Job* 2.73 *ad finem*).

5 In Luke 10:30, about the man who fell among thieves, it says: 'they departed, leaving him half dead'. The commentary: 'they stripped him of immortality, but they could not deprive him of the sense of reason, so that man would be unable to have any knowledge of and to apprehend God'.

6 Augustine, also, in his book *On Soul and Spirit* similarly posits three powers, from which it follows that, if *synderesis* is a motivational power,

it must be one of them, for there is none except these which has the function of commanding us to do something. So *synderesis* must be the power which is reason, or a part of it.

Discussion:

On the question whether it is related [to us] as a part of reason, it should be said that 'reason' can be understood in a wide sense [1] as embracing every motivational power of the rational soul, and be contrasted with the soul in the sense of the life-principle, whatever kind of life it may be. For life belongs to plants, to animals with perception and with thought, and is to be alive in general. *Synderesis* will then be some part of reason, and this is how it is understood at the end of 1 Thessalonians: 'that your spirit may be kept sound, together with soul and body'. This resolves the objection which was raised on the basis of this text.

If reason is, however, taken [2] to embrace every motivational power, including the appetitive and emotional, and thus the appetitive and emotional [powers] of the perceptory soul, then, the motivational part of *synderesis* is embraced by it only to the extent that it is apprehensory. And thus the other objection, as found in the commentary on Matthew 13 and on Job 1 'and I alone remain' etc. and on Luke 10, 'they departed leaving him half dead', which says that there are just three motivational powers of the soul, is resolved.

However, if 'reason' is understood [3] so as to exclude the appetitive and emotional, although these are also called rational powers of the soul, then *synderesis* will be part of the original righteousness of man's powers, which Adam had in the state of innocence, which remained as a little light leading him to God, lest he should be turned or bent to temporal things by his entire reason. The righteousness of grace, however, was wholly dispersed by his sinful Fall. For it is established that Adam was naturally righteous by virtue of his judgement, will and emotions: this righteousness was not completely taken away. Therefore, what remained can be called *synderesis*. For that of itself murmurs back against sin and correctly contemplates and wants what is good without qualification. And each of these looks to the highest good, to which it primarily relates. It will not, accordingly, be a potentiality separated from these powers to the extent that they are pliable, but will exist in them inflexibly, the same as each one of them. And this is how the commentary of blessed Gregory [Jerome] on Ezekiel, which says that it is beyond the three powers of the soul and above the three, is to be expounded: it is beyond conceptually, but not in reality; for it is inflexible whereas they are not – flexible, so to say, in the direction of good things which are changeable, and of virtue and of vice. Hence it is said to be above them because of its worth: for what cannot in itself be bent away from desiring good and hating evil is of higher worth than what is pliant.

But if we suppose [4] the motivational powers to be reason and understanding and appetite and emotion, such that understanding is always lifting us up above to the highest good, not examining this or that good feature of deeds (for reason may be right or not right, looking at particular good and bad things in relationship to each other, and this can sometimes be called reason in accord with understanding, which is always right in itself; but there is also reason in accord with imagination, which is concerned with good things which can be laid hold of by perception, which in most cases is not right, although it may happen to be right) then *synderesis* will not be in the reason, but above, viz. in the understanding. Reason is here divided into two portions, one of which is compared to men and the other to women; *synderesis* will be neither of them, but above both and above the emotional and the appetitive, which fall under desire. In this way, what blessed Gregory [Jerome] says about Ezekiel 1, that there are four powers to which the four animals, or their faces, are analogous, is clear.

Appendix: in what sense synderesis *murmurs back in answer to sin.*

It is asked in what sense *synderesis* is said to murmur back in answer to sin. For when someone sins, it murmurs back at him; therefore he is moved about it, and then how is he so moved, since the natural will is only moved generally? Again, what effect does it have when it corrects mistakes? Since it does not draw one back, but judges what ought not to be done, this itself reveals a judgement of free choice, even though it judges against and follows up the judging will. Again, if there is a natural will in things which are natural, living and rational, but *synderesis* is only in rational beings, why then is it necessary, since the natural will does whatever *synderesis* does and not conversely? Again, what are its proper motivators: if apprehension and desire, then of what? Again, how is it called 'understanding' and whence?

Reply: I say that *synderesis* affects free choice by telling it to do good and restraining it from evil, and moves us to the general good which is found in this or that good deed. Hence it is not in itself directed to particular good deeds, but to the general [good] which is present in them. Moreover, there is no deliberative judgement in *synderesis*, only executive. For it determines the good in any particular good deed without deliberation. And although natural will may be directed to good deeds which are rational, nevertheless *synderesis* is directed to the same things, but in a different way; for natural will is present as a potentiality, not as a dispositional potentiality, whereas *synderesis* is present as a dispositional potentiality, and will is directed to other good things, but *synderesis* is not. Its effect is both upon apprehension and on desire, but more properly on desire. Moreover, that which concerns apprehension is called 'understanding'.

Whatever is easy to actualise is called a dispositional potentiality, and so *synderesis* is called a dispositional potentiality, because it is not hampered from actualisation on its own account. This, i.e. its obstruction, happens because of the disobedience of reason. Reason itself is called a dispositional potentiality, but not to the same degree, because, although it cannot be obstructed in respect of doing an action which it wants [to do] interiorly, it can be with respect to the actualisation of a judgement in a difficult matter. Moreover, *synderesis* has the same subject as natural will, but it is called '*synderesis*' because it is directed to what is rationally good and, from this point of view, reason is a dispositional potentiality. But, according to this conception, natural will is, however, not a dispositional potentiality but just a potentiality.

3 Can one sin by following synderesis?

The third question follows, viz. whether one may sin by following it or, if it is a power of the soul, whether there may be any sin in it.

A Arguments that one can:

1 *Conscientia* is sometimes mistaken, sometimes right. But in whatever power there is any mistake over what is to be done, in that power there is sin. And that *synderesis* is *conscientia* may be granted from Gregory's [Jerome's] words, when he says: 'this *conscientia*, however, when the wicked man often reaches the depths of sin, we see thrown down', and he is speaking there of *synderesis*. Therefore there is sin in *synderesis*.

2 Since the soul is punished as a whole, and eternal damnation should

only be for sin, the soul sins with its motivational powers and, hence, with *synderesis*, since *synderesis* is a motivational power.

3 Contraries spring from the same power; but virtue and vice are contraries; therefore they spring from the same power. But the virtue which is the gift of wisdom springs from the highest power of the soul; and thus, too, with *synderesis*. Therefore there is sin in the latter.

4 *Synderesis* and the impulse [to sin] are related as opposites, because they have contrary bents, the impulse to evil, *synderesis* to good: the impulse is an evil disposition, *synderesis* a dispositional potentiality for good. But there is sin in accordance with the impulse and, therefore, also in accordance with *synderesis*.

  B Arguments that one cannot:

1 To murmur in answer to sin and to consent to it are incompatible; therefore since one of them belongs as such to *synderesis* itself, the other cannot belong to it.

2 Since there is a motivational power of the plant-soul which always goes for what is pleasant to it, e.g. what is in the liver, or appetising or digestible etc., since it is concerned with nutrition, and since there are other things pertaining to the perceptory soul by which it is always set in action, e.g. imagination or the spiritual power which resides in the heart, there will similarly be a third which is always set off by what is pleasant to the rational soul, viz. the highest good. But it is agreed that this is the highest power of the soul. Therefore it must be *synderesis*.

3 *Synderesis* looks at good and evil from the point of view of general differences; for this is what differentiates it from what has to do with deliberative virtue. But sin, since it concerns deeds, occurs in particular actions as a result of omitting what is good and transgressing into what is bad. So it is not present in *synderesis*.

  Discussion:

To the question whether *synderesis* is a power in whose exercise sin may be present in the soul, and similarly whether, in its exercise, there may be merit, it should be said that if *synderesis* is a power of the soul along with the aforesaid powers, but differing from them in the way it works, then we should hold that there is no sin in the exercise, as such, of *synderesis*, but that it helps us to merit, just as a disproportionate sensuality entices us to lose merit. However, there can happen to be merit or loss of merit in the exercise of that potentiality in another way, and this occurs to the extent that it is pliable in the direction both of good and of evil.

But if *synderesis* is the same as understanding, or as the latter together with a disposition, it should be said that there is no sin in its exercise in so far as it *is* just its own exercise, though [sin] occurs when it is deposed and the lower part [of the soul] prevents it from having its effect (as people say, 'it is clouded over by sin'), this sin being of free choice. It is clouded over because, since all the powers order things by their way [of action] in the direction of merit and, in the case of a sin of free choice, whose role is to merit by grace, all are deprived of merit and incur the penalty of sin, *synderesis* is thus clouded over by the lower part [of the soul] in sin, and is always that much less able to attain its effect the more sin is intended.

Replies to the arguments that one can sin by following synderesis:

A1 To the objection that *conscientia* can be now right, now mistaken, and if mistaken is undeserving but if right deserving, it should be said that *conscientia* comes from the conjunction of *synderesis* with free choice and is not *synderesis* itself, and is related as knowledge in action is related to knowledge in general and to knowledge from reason proper, as being between them. For example, suppose that it is written in *synderesis* that everyone who makes himself out to be the son of God and is not, should die the death; but that this man (pointing to Christ) makes himself out to be the son of God, yet is not; it is then supposed: therefore he should die the death. What was contributed by *synderesis* was unchangeable and dictated only good, but this conjoined with what was contributed by reason dictated sin. So, therefore, *synderesis* plus the reason for a free choice makes *conscientia* right or mistaken, and *conscientia* sticks more to the side of reason; *synderesis* itself, however, which is the spark of *conscientia*, as blessed Gregory says, is not mistaken.

A2 To the objection about the penalty of the soul as a whole, it is true that it is punished for not attaining its goal and means to that goal, and it is precisely because of this that it racks the soul by murmuring in answer to sin and torments itself with the pain of sin, but it does not, because of this, sin in itself, since no penalty is owing to it in the first place.

A3 To the objection that the gift of wisdom is contained in *synderesis*, since it is in the highest power of the soul, it is to be said that gifts and virtues are in the reason and will, strictly speaking, and the gift of wisdom is in the higher part of reason, and in that there can be sin, since it does not seem to be without the grace and light of God. If, however, we say that wisdom is in *synderesis*, it does not follow from this that sin in itself may be in it. For when the soul sins through one of its powers, it is deprived of the gifts of every power and, thus, although it may not sin in relation to this one, it can be deprived in relation to this one of wisdom, which is a gift of grace.

4 *Can* synderesis *be extinguished?*

There follows the fourth question, whether *synderesis* can be extinguished, so that it does not murmur in answer to sin.

A *Arguments that it can:*

1 That it may be, is seen in the arch-heretics to whom their *conscientia* dictated that they should undergo martyrdom to defend their faith. But this is a sinful mistake. Therefore *synderesis* did not murmur in them in answer to sin.

2 It also seems to be so from the commentary on Ezekiel, where it says: 'we see that this *conscientia* is cast down, when the wicked man reaches the depths of sin, and loses its place.' But what is it for it to lose its place, except for it not always to be against sin, but sometimes to sin? Therefore, since it is altogether irrecoverably thrown down in the damned, it must be extinguished in them, since they are willing to sin, though not to be punished.

3 It is said in Jeremiah 2:16: 'the children of Memphis and of Taphnes have devoured you, even to the crown of the head'. The commentary: 'The evil spirit reaches from the lower members of the body right up to the crown of the head, when the disease of despair corrupts the pure loftiness of the mind.'

4 In the Lamentations of Jeremiah 1:5, 'Her foes have become the head.'

5 On Psalm 14:1, 'they are corrupt and are made abominable', the commentary says: 'deprived of all power of reason'.

6 *Synderesis* and the impulse to sin are related as opposites because of their different tendencies. But the impulse [to sin] can be totally extinguished through the fulness of grace, as in the blessed Virgin and in Christ. Therefore *synderesis* can be wholly extinguished in some of the reprobate, e.g. in anti-Christ, by a pile of wickedness.

7 On Psalm 56:3, 'From the height [of the day I shall fear]: but I will trust in you', the commentary says: 'there are three conditions of the body, health, which perceives, dulness, which does not perceive, immortality, which does not perceive, but in different ways. Similarly there are three in the soul.' Hence there can be a dulness in the soul so that it does not actually discern spiritually. Therefore the exercise of *synderesis* is thus extinguished in it.

B *Arguments that it cannot:*

1 Against this is what is said at the end of Isaiah (66:24), 'their worm shall not die' etc. But that worm is *conscientia*, which is always contrary to sin.

2 In the Book of Wisdom (5:3,8) it is said: 'They will speak to one another in repentance: what has our arrogance profited us?'

3 About Lazarus, whom the rich man in hell begged to be sent to him, so that from the touch of the end of his finger dipped in water he might feel some coolness, where Luke (16:28) says 'I have five brothers', etc., the commentary explains: 'After hope is taken away from the one who is burning, the mind turns to its near kindred because pain sometimes instructs the mind of the reprobate to love uselessly, so that they love their kin in the spirit, although here they loved sin and did not love themselves.' Therefore it begs good for itself and for others. Therefore *synderesis* does not appear to have been extinguished in it.

4 Blessed Bernard, in his book *On Free Choice*: 'How should something

not have savour when, through evils which are endured, people are forced to repent of their bad deeds?' Therefore they have an impulse to what is good.

Discussion and replies to arguments:

To resolve what has been said, a distinction must be drawn: one thing applies to those who *have been* changed, another to those who *may be* damned [i.e. are still on life's journey]. Hence:

A1 To the objection from the example of the arch-heretics, whether *synderesis* murmurs in them in answer to sin, since *conscientia* dictates to them that they ought to undergo martyrdom to defend their faith, it should be said that, in accordance with the above, the effect of *synderesis*, considered as such, is paralysed in them because of the lack of faith, which is the basis of everything good. But the exercise of *conscientia* thrives in them, the evidence of which is that the man is ready to undergo martyrdom, because he supposes what he believes to be the faith. It is not, however, *synderesis* which does this, but what belongs to free choice or reason. Moreover, *synderesis* is not extinguished in such a person because, although he may be mistaken about the particular matter, evil in general still displeases him, mistakes [in general] still displease him, and this is in accordance with *synderesis*. This is shown by the conversion of many, upon recognising their mistake. Thus Ambrose says, about Augustine's remark to his mother, 'Let it be, because he will discover by reading what a great mistake it is.' And it is like someone who knows in general that every she-mule is sterile, and yet believes that this she-mule is pregnant; when he studies and thinks it over, the mistake goes away and, knowing that it is a she-mule and thinking over his general [knowledge], he knows that it is not pregnant.

A2–4 To the objection that 'we see this *conscientia* to be thrown down' etc., it should be said that it can happen that it is deposed, i.e. is over-clouded by sin, but not extinguished. The objection from Jeremiah 2, 'the children of Memphis' etc., is resolved by the commentary, which says about it: 'the crown of the head is corrupted, when faith is corrupted', where the crown of the head is expounded as faith. The other text, from Lamentations 1, 'Her foes have become the head', is expounded in terms of intention. And 'they are corrupt' etc., is said in virtue of the power of reason.

A6 The reply to the next objection is that it is otherwise with *synderesis* from the impulse [to sin], because the impulse [to sin] is a disposition, *synderesis* a dispositional potentiality, and thus psychologically more basic. Yet it is true that the impulse [to sin] is to some extent inextinguishable, with respect to what is painful, as is hunger and thirst; but with respect to fault and to tendency to evil, it may be extinguished, as in the most blessed Virgin.

A7 The reply to the following objection is that there can be dulness in the soul, but that *synderesis* cannot be extinguished by this kind of dulness. Thus three things are distinguished in the commentary quoted: 'a foreseen precaution', which corresponds to health, 'foolish presumption', which corresponds to dulness, 'secure glory', which corresponds to immortality. Hence the commentary goes on to say: 'Foolish presumption is like dulness when someone, anticipating how he will behave, neither fears nor takes care', and thus it takes away fear. And elsewhere we find that the irregularity of sin takes away sadness: so in Ephesians 4:19 we read 'Who, despairing, have given themselves up to lewdness' and another text says about this: 'insensitive to pain, that is, not being pained by their sins'. However, it is not proved by this that the exercise of *synderesis* is taken away, for grief for sin and fear and taking precaution pertain to free choice and, although these may be taken away, the exercise of *synderesis* can remain, just as, in men who are disabled with paralysed members, the internal working of the heart and breathing of the lungs thrives.

B3 To the objection about the rich man and Lazarus, the effects of *synderesis* in impelling to good are to be distinguished from those in making us displeased with evil – and the latter doubly distinguished, either in connection with guilt or outside this context. It should be said, therefore, that *synderesis*, as impelling to good and as making us displeased without qualification about evil faults, is extinguished in the devil and in the damned. But in the third way, it is not extinguished, and this remains as guilt. This is clear from the other part of the commentary on this section of Luke 16: 'The rich man is delivered to pain and discernment [of the state] of the poor man whom he despised, and the memory of the brothers whom he had left, in order that he may be the more fully racked by the sight of the glory of the one he had despised and by the punishment of those whom he loved in vain.' And it is about this that it is said at the end of Isaiah 'their worm shall not die', etc. They are, therefore, displeased with evil in connection with its penalty. This is remarked in the petition of the rich man, for he begs that it should be told [to his brothers] lest they should come to this place of torments: he does this so that they shall not do deeds worthy of eternal punishment and does it so they shall not come to this place of torments. And thus it is the work of *synderesis* which sin, taken in conjunction with its penalty, displeases.

B4 To the other argument, in the book of blessed Bernard *On Free Choice*, 'How should something not have savour when ...?' etc., he himself replies by adding: 'They wholly wish not to be punished, but it is just to be punished for deeds which ought to be punished' where 'the will which does not accord with justice is bad' and subsequently 'they do not truly repent who grieve less that they have lived thus, than that now they cannot do so'.

Bonaventure (1221–1274)

John of Fidanza was born near Viterbo and took the name 'Bonaventure' when he became a Franciscan about 1238. He was educated and subsequently taught at the University of Paris until 1257, when he became minister general of the Franciscans. His commentary on Peter Lombard's Judgements, from which the treatise on conscience translated below is taken, was written between 1250 and 1255. Later works include Old Testament commentaries and The Journey of the Mind towards God.

COMMENTARY ON PETER LOMBARD'S 'BOOKS OF JUDGEMENTS' 2.39

(Latin text in *S. Bonaventurae, Opera omnia*, vol. 2. *Ad Claras Aquas* (Quaracchi), *ex typographia Collegii S. Bonaventurae*, 1885, pp. 898–915.) I have omitted all but four of the objections and replies.

1 Conscientia

1.1 Does conscientia *belong to the thinking or to the desiring part of the soul?*

> *Arguments that it belongs to the desiring part:*

3 According to what John of Damascus says, 'the law of the flesh is opposed to the law of the mind' (*On the Orthodox Faith* 95). But the law of the flesh belongs to the motivational part [of the soul]; therefore the law of the mind also belongs to the same part. But '*conscientia* is the law of the mind', as John of Damascus says. Therefore *conscientia* belongs to the desiring part.

> *Discussion:*

Just as the word 'thought' sometimes means the potentiality of thinking, sometimes the disposition and sometimes the idea which is thought about, so too the word '*conscientia*' usually has three meanings for the teachers of holy Scripture. Sometimes '*conscientia*' means the thing of which we are conscious; in this sense, John of Damascus says that '*conscientia* is the law of our thought' (*On the Orthodox Faith* 95), since a law is what we recognise by means of *conscientia*. Sometimes, however, '*conscientia*' means the potentiality of being conscious, for example, as it is said that the natural law is written in our *conscientiae*. But although '*conscientia*' is wont to have three meanings, the more usual sense of the word is for the disposition, as of the word 'knowledge' (*scientia*), of which it is a compound.

If, then, it be asked of what potentiality it is a disposition, it should be said that it is a disposition of the potentiality of apprehension, but in a different way from theoretical knowledge, because theoretical knowledge perfects our thought to the extent that the latter is theoretical, whereas *conscientia* is a disposition perfecting our thought to the extent that it is practical, or to the extent that it directs us towards deeds. And thus thought has a motivational aspect, not because it effects change, but because it tells us to do something and turns us towards doing it. Such a disposition is, accordingly, not just called 'knowledge' (*scientia*), but '*conscientia*', so as to signify that this disposition does not in itself perfect the theoretical potentiality, but does so as joined in some way to desire and deed. Because of this, we do not say that *conscientia* dictates premisses like 'every whole is greater than any of its parts', but rightly say that it tells us 'God is to be honoured' and similar premisses, which are like rules for what is to be done.

It is therefore to be admitted, as the arguments show, that *conscientia* lies in the apprehensory potentiality, although it does not lie in the latter *qua* theoretical, but *qua* practical. 'For speculative and practical thought are said to be the same potentiality, differing only in their extension' (Aristotle, *De anima* 3.7,431^{b}10–12); nor can it be in any way supposed that practical thought is desire or will: Aristotle himself denies this.

Replies to arguments that it belongs to the desiring part:

3 To the objection that the law of the flesh is opposed to the law of the mind it should be said, with Master Hugh of St Victor, that in sensuality or the external man there is not only corruption with respect to the motivational and inclining potentiality, but also with respect to the perceptory [potentiality] (*On the Sacraments* 1.7.34). Hence, although the law of the flesh consists mainly in an appetite tending towards evil,

it nevertheless presupposes imaginative and apprehensory [potentiali-ties] representing fleshly things in a disordered way. These two [potentialities] must similarly be taken into account in relation to the law of the mind. *Conscientia*, however, is in itself directly opposed to the law of the flesh more by reason of the preliminary apprehension than by reason of appetite.

1.2 Is conscientia *an innate or an acquired disposition?*

Apart from the position taken by Plato, who supposed that every apprehensory disposition is innate to the soul without qualification, but is temporarily forgotten because of the burden of the body, a view which both Aristotle and Augustine disprove and criticise, there were three learned opinions about the origin of apprehensory dispositions. All three opinions agree that just as virtues which are a matter of habit are neither wholly derived from nature nor wholly acquired, but partly innate and partly acquired, so also apprehensory dispositions are neither wholly innate nor wholly acquired, but partly innate and partly acquired. They differ, however, in the ways in which they regard these dispositions as being innate and as being acquired.

Some people want to say that they are innate with respect to the active intellect but acquired with respect to the possible intellect; and that, about the latter, Aristotle says that the soul is created like a blank sheet of paper and that this intellect is perfected by means of the per-ceptory powers (*De anima* 3.4,429^{b}30–430^{a}2). But this does not appear to accord either with Aristotle's words or with the truth. For if the active intellect had apprehensory dispositions, why could it not com-municate them to the possible intellect without the aid of the lower senses? Moreover, if the active intellect had apprehensory dispositions, the soul would already, from its very state, not be ignorant but, rather, would have knowledge. It is also difficult to see how, on this view, the forms are said to be in the active intellect, since the possible intellect is said to be 'that by which it [the intellect] can become everything' and the active 'that by which it can make everything' (*De anima* 3.5,430^a 14–15).

Hence there is a second way of saying that apprehensory dispositions are partly innate and partly acquired. Namely, they are innate with respect to apprehension in general, but acquired with respect to appre-hension of the particular; or innate with respect to the apprehension of premises but acquired with respect to the apprehension of conclusions;

so that an axiom is what everyone approves just on hearing it. But this way of speaking, too, agrees neither with the words of Aristotle nor of Augustine. For Aristotle proves that apprehension of premises is not innate to us by inferring many difficulties from such an assumption (*Posterior Analytics* 2.19, 99ᵇ22 ff) and he shows there that 'apprehension of premises is acquired from perception, memory and experience'. Augustine, also, talking of the child in Plato's *Meno* who answered questions about all the premises of geometry, says that this was not because the soul of the child knew them beforehand, but rather 'he saw these things by a sort of incorporeal light of an unique kind; as the eye of the flesh sees things adjacent to itself in this bodily light, of which light it is made to be receptive, and adapted to it' (*On the Trinity* 12.15).

There is thus a third way of saying that apprehensory dispositions are partly innate and partly acquired, not just by speaking about apprehension of the particular and about apprehension of conclusions, but also about apprehension of premises. For since it is necessary to apprehension that two things should be present concurrently, namely what can be apprehended and light by means of which we judge the former, as we see in the case of sight and as Augustine suggests in the passage quoted above, apprehensory dispositions are partly innate because of a light imparted to the soul, but also partly acquired because of forms. This accords with the words both of Aristotle and of Augustine. For everyone agrees that there is an imparted light of the apprehensory potentiality which is called a natural tribunal, but we acquire forms and likenesses of things by means of the senses, as Aristotle says explicitly in many places (*Posterior Analytics* 1.18; 2.15; *De anima* 3.8; *Metaphysics* 1.1) and as experience also teaches us. For no one would ever apprehend *whole* or *part*, or *father* or *mother*, unless he received its form through one of the external senses; thus it is that 'losing one of our senses, we necessarily have to lose one [branch of] knowledge' (Aristotle, *Posterior Analytics* 1.18, 81ᵃ38–39). However, that light or natural tribunal directs the soul itself in judging both of what can be apprehended and of what can be done.

But the following point is to be especially noted. Just as certain things which can be apprehended are exceedingly plain, e.g. axioms and primary premises, but some things are less plain, e.g. particular conclusions; so, too, some things which can be done are maximally plain, e.g. 'Do not do to others what you do not want to be done to you' (Tobias 4:16; cf. Matthew 7:12, Luke 6:31), that one ought to submit to God, and so on. Apprehension of basic premises is therefore said to

be innate to us in virtue of that light, because that light is enough to
apprehend them by, once the forms have been assimilated, without any
further persuasion, on account of their own clarity. Thus apprehension
of the basic premises of behaviour is innate to us, in that the ability to
judge is enough to apprehend them by. Moreover, apprehension of the
particular conclusions of [the various branches of] knowledge is
acquired in that the light which is innate to us is not enough to apprehend them, but demands some persuasion and a new aptitude. This is
also to be understood as applying to deeds, which are things to be done
and to which we are bound, which we only apprehend by additional
education.

Since 'conscientia' thus names a disposition which directs our judgement with respect to what can be done, it follows that in one way it
names an innate disposition with regard to basic dictates of nature, but
an acquired disposition with regard to what is added by education. It
also betokens an innate disposition with respect to a directing light, but
an acquired disposition with respect to the form of what is itself apprehensible. For I have a natural light which is enough to apprehend that
one's parents are to be honoured and that one's neighbours are not to be
harmed, but I do not have the form of *father* or form of *neighbour*
naturally impressed upon me.

1.3 Are we bound to do everything which conscientia tells us to be necessary to salvation?

Conscientia sometimes tells us what is in accordance with the law of
God, sometimes what is in addition to the law of God and sometimes
what is against the law of God – we are speaking here of what it tells us
by way of prescription or proscription, not by way of advice or persuasion. In the first case, *conscientia* binds without qualification and
generally, in that a man is bound to such things by divine law; and
conscientia, which accords with it, manifests the bond. In the second case,
conscientia binds so long as it persists, so that a man must either change
his *conscientia* or must carry out what it tells him, e.g. if it tells him that
it is necessary to salvation to pick up a stalk from the ground. In the
third case *conscientia* does not bind us to act or not to act, but binds us to
change it, because, since such a *conscientia* is mistaken and the mistake is
incompatible with the divine law, so long as it persists it necessarily
places a man outside the state of salvation. It is therefore necessary to
change it, since whether a man does what it says or the opposite, he sins

mortally. For if he does what his *conscientia* tells him, and that is against the law of God, and to act against the law of God is mortal sin, then without any doubt he sins mortally. But if he does the opposite of what his *conscientia* tells him, the latter persisting, he still sins mortally, not in virtue of the deed which he does but because he does it in an evil way. For he does it in despite of God, so long as he believes, his *conscientia* telling him so, that this displeases God, although [in fact] it pleases God. And this is what the commentary on Romans 14:23, 'Everything which does not issue from faith is sin', says: 'The apostle says that everything which is a matter of conscience, if done otherwise, is a sin. For although one may also do what is good, if one believes that it ought not to be done, it is a sin.' The reason for this is that God does not merely take notice of *what* a man does, but with what intention (*quo animo*) he does it, and the man who does what God commands, believing himself to be acting against the will of God, does not do it with a good intention and therefore sins mortally.

It is thus clear that *conscientia* always either binds us to do what it tells us, or binds us to change it. *Conscientia* does not, however, always bind us to do what it tells us, e.g. a *conscientia* which tells us that we are not obliged to do something to which a man would, otherwise, be bound. Such a *conscientia* is called 'mistaken'.

2 *Synderesis*

2.1 *Is* synderesis *to be classified with apprehension or with desire?*

There are manifold views about the distinction of *synderesis* from the other powers, as about the differences between the other powers of the soul. Some people wanted to say – basing themselves on the commentary on Ezekiel 1 – that *synderesis* is the highest [part] of the soul. The highest [part] of the soul, however, is the higher part of reason, by which the soul is turned towards God, and this higher part rules the lower part of reason, and the emotional and appetitive [parts of the soul]. But this higher part, when turned towards God, is always right, though it is turned aside when it comes down to these lower [parts]. These people said that the difference between *synderesis* and *conscientia* and natural law is that '*synderesis*' names the potentiality, i.e. the higher part [of reason], '*conscientia*' names a disposition of it, by which it regulates the lower part, and 'natural law' names that to which *conscientia* directs itself. This way of talking seems to be probable enough, unless it should be incompatible with the commentary mentioned, which says that *synderesis* does not get mixed up with the other sinning [powers]. For since mortal sin cannot occur without an actualisation of the higher part [of reason], because the fulness of sin consists in the man's eating [reference to Adam], if *synderesis* were the higher part of reason, it would at least be involved with the other sinning [powers]. Moreover, the higher part of reason implies a directing towards God, whereas the actualisation of *synderesis* concerns not only God, but also our neighbour, since natural law covers both.

And so there is another account, to the effect that, since the rational potentialities can be deployed in two ways, viz. by thought and by desire, both naturally and through deliberation, so, just as freedom of choice depends upon reason and will because it works by deliberation, similarly *conscientia* and *synderesis* look to reason and will, because they work naturally. (*Synderesis* as much as *conscientia*, and also natural law, always turn to what is good, but free choice sometimes turns to what is good, sometimes to what is bad.) And therefore, just as free choice simultaneously embraces reason and will, so *synderesis* simultaneously embraces reason and will, and similarly natural law, and similarly *conscientia*, and they can be taken as being the same. *Synderesis* is, however, appropriately called a potentiality, *conscientia* a disposition and the natural law their object, or, according to another classification, *synderesis* is a disposition with respect to good and bad in general, *conscientia* a disposition with respect to good or bad in particular, and natural law is related indifferently to either. But because, as was argued above, *conscientia* is an intellectual disposition, either it is necessary to suppose that there is something over and above *conscientia* and *synderesis* which directs us, or it is necessary to suppose that *synderesis* is in the desiring part [of the soul].

Hence there is a third account, to the effect that just as the intellectual part [of the soul] has, since its very creation, a light which is a natural tribunal for it, directing the intellect towards what can be apprehended, so too desire has a certain natural bias, directing it to what is desirable. There are two kinds of thing which are desirable: some are honourable, others useful, just as there are two kinds of thing which can be apprehended, some being theoretical, some to do with behaviour. And just as '*conscientia*' only names judgement which is directed to behaviour, so '*synderesis*' only names that bias of the will, or the will with that bias, which makes it turn to good things which are honourable. And just as the word '*conscientia*' can mean the potentiality with such a disposition, or the disposition of such a potentiality, so too '*synderesis*'. In the more usual sense, though, '*synderesis*' means a dispositional potentiality rather than a disposition, as can be seen from the authorities who have been quoted above. And because this potentiality is never separated from that disposition, it follows that disposition and potentiality are included in one term and that this potentiality, so disposed, is classified under the name of its disposition.

2.2 Can synderesis *be extinguished by sin?*

Arguments that it can:

4 The impulse [to sin] is the opposite of *synderesis*; but the impulse [to sin] may be totally extinguished, as appears in the blessed Virgin [Mary]. It seems, therefore, that *synderesis* may similarly be extinguished by a host of sins.

Discussion:

The exercise of *synderesis* can be prevented, but it cannot be extinguished. It cannot be extinguished because, as it is something natural, it cannot be taken away from us altogether. Hence the commentary on Luke 10:30, 'they departed, leaving him half dead', says: 'they stripped him of immortality, but they could not deprive him of the sense of reason, so that man would be unable to have any knowledge of and to apprehend God', 'nor does vice ever wipe out the last traces of nature'.

However, although its exercise cannot be taken away or extinguished altogether, it can be temporarily prevented, either by the darkness of blindness, or by the wantonness of pleasure, or by the hardness of obstinacy. *Synderesis* is hampered by the darkness of blindness so that it does not murmur in reply to evil, because the evil is believed to be good, as e.g. in the case of heretics who, while dying for the impiety of their error, believe that they die for their piety of faith, so that they feel no guilt but, instead, a fictitious and vain joy. Similarly, it is hampered by the wantonness of pleasure, for sometimes in sins of the flesh a man is so engrossed by the exercise of the flesh that a sense of guilt has no place, because men of the flesh are so far carried away by the impulse to pleasure that reason has then no place [in them]. *Synderesis* is also hampered by the hardness of obstinacy, so that it does not goad us into [doing] good, as e.g. in the case of the damned, who are so strongly reinforced in evil that they can never turn towards what is good.

Thus *synderesis* is perpetually hampered from goading us to do good and, consequently, can be said to be extinguished in respect of its exercise, but not extinguished without qualification, because it has another use, namely, to murmur in reply [to evil]. In this use, in which the function of *synderesis* is to sting and murmur in reply to evil, it flourishes most in the damned. I say this, in the sense in which murmuring in reply to evil is a punishment, not in the sense in which it is a matter of justice, because this murmuring in reply will be a commendation of divine justice but will not have the purpose of bringing forth fruitful repentance. Hence, in the damned, *synderesis* murmurs in reply to their guilt, yet in relation to punishment.

Replies to arguments that synderesis *can be extinguished by sin:*

4 The reply to the objection concerning the impulse [to sin] is that it is not like [*synderesis*], because the impulse [to sin] is a faulty condition contrary to nature, and so can be totally removed while yet preserving nature, whereas it is not so with *synderesis*. For the latter belongs to the first arrangement of nature and this cannot be altogether taken away while preserving nature. There is also another reason, that there is a grace or gift of grace, given as a favour, which is directly opposed to the impulse [to sin] and which removes the corruption of the flesh. But vice and sin are not to be found in connection with the actualisation of *synderesis*; and so, however much a man may have sinned, there yet remain in him both *conscientia* and *synderesis*.

2.3 Can synderesis *be corrupted by sin?*

Arguments that it can:

2 On Jeremiah 2:16, 'The children of Memphis', etc., the commentary says: 'The evil spirit reaches from the lower members to the crown when the disease of despair corrupts the pure loftiness of the mind.' But *synderesis* is itself the pure loftiness of the mind; therefore it may be corrupted by sin.

4 *Synderesis* follows on from *conscientia* as its natural tribunal (cf. 2.1). But *conscientia* may be right or mistaken. It seems, necessarily, therefore,

that *synderesis* is sometimes moved straightforwardly, sometimes moved deviantly. If, then, the disorder found in the actualisation by which it is moved is blameworthy, it seems [that *synderesis* can be corrupted by sin].

Discussion:

According to those who say that *synderesis* is no other than the higher part of reason, there may happen to be sin in its exercise. For they say that this higher part of reason works in two ways: either by being turned to God and being ruled and directed by eternal laws, in which case there is no sin in it, or by being turned to the lower powers, in which case it may take occasion to be turned out of the way by them and can be corrupted by sin. They cite the sin of Arius as an example, who was mistaken about the Trinity and Unity [of God], and thus in the higher part of reason or in *synderesis*. And this, they say, is what the commentary on Ezekiel 1 means: for it says, first, that 'it does not get mixed up with the other sinning [powers]' and afterwards, that 'it is cast down and loses its place'. Both of these remarks, they say, are true in accordance with different comparisons of the higher part of reason or *synderesis*.

But since, as the saints and the commentary clearly say, the proper job of *synderesis* is always to goad us into doing good and to murmur in reply to sin, as long as we remain alive, other writers said something different, namely, that '*synderesis*' names the will in so far as the latter works naturally. And since there is no sin in the actualisation of will as [part of our] nature, or as it works naturally, but only when it works deliberatively, it follows that *synderesis* cannot be corrupted by sin. Because, however, it has the job of regulating and directing the other [powers] and can lose the power to regulate them, it follows that it can be overthrown by our fault. For its power of government depends upon two factors, namely, on the rightness of its government and on the obedience of its service and, although *synderesis* is always right in itself, it is said, because reason and will often go against it – reason by the blindness of error and will by the obstinacy of impiety – to be overthrown, in that its effect and its government of the other deliberative powers is repulsed and broken. The example of a soldier is cited, who, so far as it lies in himself, always sits well on a horse but, if the horse falls, is said to be overthrown. And that is how [the overthrow of *synderesis*] is to be understood.

Replies to arguments that synderesis *can be corrupted by sin:*

2 In reply to the objection that the disease of despair corrupts the loftiness of the mind and that the soul is utterly debauched right up to its
crown, it is to be said that it is not *synderesis*, but the higher part of
reason, which is there called the 'crown' or 'loftiness' of the mind. The
higher part of reason, however, does not name that potentiality of the
soul in which it is moved *naturally*, but in which it is moved *deliberatively*. And it is in this way that sin can befall it, especially the kind
which is to be found in the superior actualisation of reason, as are the
sins of unbelief and despair, and other sins which are directly opposed to
the theological virtues.

4 In reply to the objection that *conscientia*, which is the tribunal pre-
ceding *synderesis*, is right and not right, and therefore also *synderesis*, it
is to be said that this does not follow, because *conscientia* does not just
consist in the general, but also descends to the particular; it is not only
moved by simple movement, but also by comparing. This is not surprising, because it consists in reason, whose job is to distinguish one
thing from another and to compare one thing with another. And thus,
although *conscientia* is always right so long as it sticks to the general and
is moved by simple inspection, it can become mistaken when it descends
to particulars and brings things together, because the actualisation of
deliberative reason is mixed with it.

This will be clear from the following. The *conscientia* of the Jews first
told them itself by natural pronouncement that God is to be obeyed,
and they assumed henceforth that God *now* directs circumcision and
keeping [certain] foods separate. From this their *conscientia* is formed in
the particular [matter], that they should circumcise themselves and
abstain from [certain] foods. This mistake does not come from the first
premiss, which was indeed true, but comes from adding the minor
premiss, which was not from *conscientia* as a natural tribunal, but rather
from mistaken reason, which has regard to free choice. But *synderesis* is
in itself moved by a simple movement when it murmurs back against
evil and prods us to good. Moreover, it is not moved against this or
that evil, but in general; or if *synderesis* is turned in some way to hate
this or that evil, it is not in so far as it is *this*, but in so far as it is *evil*. And
thus it is that *synderesis* does not deviate in the way that *conscientia* makes
mistakes.

Another reason can also be given, that '*synderesis*' names the natural potentiality, as it is naturally adapted [to us], whereas '*conscientia*' names a disposition which is not just natural but also acquired; and that nature is always, in itself, rightly moved, whereas what is acquired may fall under rightness or under deviance. Hence, although *synderesis* always exists rightly, *conscientia* may be right or mistaken.

Aquinas (1225–1274)

Thomas of Aquino was born at Roccasecca near Naples and sent as a child to the abbey of Monte Cassino. At 14 he became a student at the newly-founded University of Naples and then, after joining the Dominicans in 1244, at their college in Paris, where he was taught by Albert the Great. He became Master of Theology in 1256 and taught at the University of Paris for three years, then in various Italian cities from 1259–1268, returning to Paris in 1268 and teaching there again until 1272. In 1272 he was given the job of organising the Dominican college at the University of Naples and died two years later on his way to the Council of Lyons. He wrote commentaries on most of Aristotle's philosophical works, on Peter Lombard's Books of 'Judgements', some biblical commentaries, two theological text-books and other commentaries and treatises. He also wrote up many of his seminar courses, among which is the one on conscience translated here.

DEBATED QUESTIONS ON TRUTH 16–17

(Latin text in *S. Thomae Aquinatis, Opera omnia*, vol. 22. *Quaestiones disputatae de veritate.* Rome: ad Sancta Sabinae, 1972, pp. 501–528.) Most of the objections and replies and the whole of 17.5 have been omitted here.

16 Synderesis

16.1 Is synderesis a potentiality or a disposition?

Arguments that it is a potentiality:

7 *Synderesis* is opposed to sensuality, because *synderesis* always tends towards what is good just as sensuality always tends towards what is bad. But sensuality is a pure potentiality without any disposition; hence so is *synderesis*.

9 'Higher reason' names a pure potentiality. But it appears that *synderesis* is the same as higher reason, for Augustine says: 'Those rules and

insights pertaining to the virtues, and which are both true and unchangeable, are present in the natural tribunal which we call "*synderesis*" (*On Free Choice* 2.10). According to Augustine, however, it is the
part of higher reason to hold fast to unchangeable notions (*On the
Trinity* 12.2,7). Therefore *synderesis* is a pure potentiality.

11 Contraries cannot be in the same thing. But the impulse [to sin],
which always tends towards what is bad, is innate to us. Therefore there
cannot be any disposition in us which always tends to what is good, and
hence *synderesis*, which always tends to what is good, is neither a disposition nor a disposition with a potentiality, but is a pure potentiality.

13 If *synderesis* were a potentiality with a disposition, it would not be a
passive, but an active potentiality, since something would count as its
exercise. However, an active potentiality is based upon a form, just as a
passive one on matter. But there is a double form in the human soul:
one, which is higher, through which it belongs with the angels, in
virtue of being spirit; another, which is lower, through which it gives
life to the body, in virtue of being soul. *Synderesis*, therefore, must be
based either upon the higher form or upon the lower. If upon the
higher, then it is higher reason: if upon the lower, then it is lower
reason. But higher just as much as lower reason is a pure potentiality.
Hence *synderesis* [is a pure potentiality].

15 The job of *synderesis* seems to be to judge; that is why it is called a
'natural tribunal'. But free choice (*arbitrium*) gets its name from judging.
So free choice is the same as *synderesis*. But free choice is a pure potentiality. Therefore [*synderesis* is a pure potentiality].

Discussion:

There are different opinions on this question. Some people say that
synderesis is a potentiality, without qualification, other than reason and
superior to it. Others say that although it is a potentiality, without
qualification, it is in fact the same as reason, but is thought of as if it
were different. For reason is thought of as such to the extent that it
reasons about and compares things; thus it is called the 'rational power'.
But it is also thought of as a nature, to the extent that it naturally
apprehends things and, from this point of view, it is called '*synderesis*'.
Yet others say that *synderesis* is the potentiality of reason allied to a

natural disposition. Which of these views is the more correct, we shall see in what follows.

As pseudo-Denis says, divine wisdom joins together the boundaries of what is prior with the beginnings of what is secondary (*On the Divine Names* 7), because inter-related natures are like contiguous bodies of which the upper part of the lower body touches the lower part of the upper body. Thus a lower nature, at its highest, comes near to what is proper to a higher nature, participating in the latter imperfectly. Now the nature of the human mind is below that of an angel, if we consider what is the natural way for either to apprehend things. It is proper to the nature of an angel to apprehend the truth without inquiry or running over the matter, but proper to human nature to reach an apprehension of truth by inquiring and by running from one point to another. As a result, the human mind, at its highest, comes near to something of what is proper to an angelic nature, i.e. by apprehending some things immediately and without inquiry although, in this, it is inferior to an angel because it only apprehends the truth in such cases through the senses.

However, two kinds of apprehension are found in the nature of an angel: theoretical, by which it contemplates the very truth of a matter simply and without qualification; and practical, as is held both by philosophers who assume that angels move the stars and planets and that all natural forms pre-exist in their apprehension, and by theologians, who assume that angels serve God in spiritual offices, in accordance with which their ranks are distinguished. Thus in human nature, in so far as it comes near to that of angels, there must be apprehension of the truth without inquiry both in theoretical and in practical matters. Moreover, this apprehension must be the source of all subsequent apprehension, whether theoretical or practical, since sources should be more stable and certain. So this apprehension must be naturally present in man, because he apprehends it as a kind of seed-bed of all subsequent knowledge, just as the natural germs of subsequent behaviour and effects pre-exist in every nature. This apprehension must also be dispositional, so that it will be ready for use when needed.

Accordingly, just as there is a natural disposition of the human mind by which it apprehends the principles of theoretical disciplines, which we call the understanding of principles, so too it has a natural disposition concerned with the basic principles of behaviour, which are the general principles of natural law. This disposition relates to *synderesis*; it exists in no other potentiality but reason (unless, perhaps, we assume that intelligence is a distinct potentiality from reason; but I have already argued against this in 15.1). We may therefore conclude that '*synderesis*' either names a natural disposition, without qualification, comparable to the disposition by which theoretical principles are apprehended, or names the potentiality of reason endowed with such a disposition. It does not make much difference which, because only the meaning of the word is at issue. However, if the potentiality of reason itself, as it naturally apprehends things, be called '*synderesis*', it cannot be so-called minus every disposition, because natural apprehension belongs to reason along with some natural disposition, as is clear from the example of understanding theoretical principles.

Replies to arguments that synderesis *is a potentiality:*

7 It is through corruption by the impulse [to sin] that sensuality always tends towards what is bad, and that corruption is there by way of a disposition. So, too, *synderesis* always tends towards what is good by a natural disposition.

9 '*Synderesis*' names neither higher nor lower reason, but something which is shared by both. For that disposition of the general premisses of law includes some which concern eternal notions, for example, that God is to be obeyed, but some which concern lower notions, for example, that one should conduct one's life rationally. *Synderesis*, however, is said to aim at unchangeable things in one sense, higher reason in another. For:

1 A thing is said to be unchangeable because its nature is unchangeable; thus divine things are unchangeable. In this sense, higher reason aims at what is unchangeable.

2 Something is also said to be unchangeable because of the necessity of its truth, although it is about things which are changeable with respect to their natures, e.g. the truth 'Every whole is greater than any of its parts' is unchangeable even in application [to changeable things]. In this sense, *synderesis* aims at what is unchangeable.

11 The innate disposition which tends towards what is bad belongs to the lower part of the soul, by which the latter is joined to the body, but the disposition which naturally tends towards what is good belongs to

the higher part of the soul. Hence these two contrary dispositions are not [dispositions] of the same [potentiality] in the same way.

13 To the extent that '*synderesis*' names a potentiality, it seems to name a passive potentiality rather than an active one. For an active potentiality is not distinguished from a passive one by having an exercise, because, since every potentiality of the soul, passive as well as active, has some exercise, every potentiality of the soul would be active. The difference is apprehended, however, by comparing the potentiality with its object. If the object is related to the potentiality as undergoing something and being changed, the potentiality will be active; but if, conversely, it is related as agent and causing change, the potentiality will be passive. Hence it is that all the potentialities of the plant-soul are active, because food is changed in growth and reproduction through a potentiality of the soul, whereas all of the perceptory potentialities are passive, because they are changed and become actualised by perceptible objects.

Now with regard to the intellect, there is an active and a passive potentiality, because what is potentially intelligible becomes actually intelligible through the intellect which is the agent intellect; so the agent intellect is an active potentiality. The thing that is actually intelligible also makes the potential intellect become actual intellect, and thus the possible intellect is a passive potentiality. However, it is not supposed that the agent intellect but, rather, that the possible is the subject of dispositions. Hence the potentiality to which a natural disposition is subject seems to be a passive rather than an active potentiality.

But even were it granted that it is an active potentiality, the argument does not continue correctly. For there are not two forms in the soul, but only one, which is its essence, because it is both spirit by its essence and is the form of the body by its essence, not by something added on. Hence higher and lower reason are not based upon two forms, but upon one essence of the soul. Moreover, it is not even true that lower reason is based upon the essence of the soul in virtue of that relationship by which it is the form of the body, for only those powers which are tied up with organs, of which lower reason is not one, are so based upon the essence of the soul.

Also, if it were granted that the potentiality which '*synderesis*' names is the same as higher or lower reason, nothing prevents us from naming the potentiality alone with the name 'reason', but naming the same [potentiality] together with an inherent disposition by the name '*synderesis*'.

15 There are two kinds of judgement:

1 of generalities: this belongs to *synderesis*.

2 of particular things that can be done: this is the judgement of selection, and belongs to free choice.

16.2 Can synderesis *do wrong?*

Arguments that it can:

1 It is said of *synderesis* in the commentary [of Jerome] on Ezekiel 1:17: 'We sometimes see that this is cast down'. But casting down, with reference to deeds, is no other than sin. Therefore [*synderesis* can do wrong].

2 Although sin is not attributable, strictly speaking, either to a disposition or to a potentiality, but to a man, because actualisations are of individuals, a disposition or potentiality is nevertheless said to sin when a man is led into sinning by the actualisation of some potentiality or disposition. But a man is sometimes led into sinning by the actualisation of *synderesis*, for it is said in John 14:2, 'The time comes when everyone who kills you will judge that he does God a service', and thus some people were disposed to killing the apostles by the judgement which they made that God's will is to be complied with, which belongs to *synderesis*. Therefore [*synderesis* can do wrong].

Discussion:

Nature, in all its works, aims at what is good and at the maintenance of whatever comes about through the working of nature. Hence, in all the works of nature, its first principles are always permanent and unchangeable and conserve right order, because first principles must endure, as Aristotle says (*Physics* 1.6, 189a19). For there could be no stability or certainty in what results from the first principles, unless the first principles were solidly established. Anything which is variable goes back, accordingly, to some first fixed thing. So it is, also, that every particular apprehension comes from some absolutely certain apprehension about which there can be no mistake. This is apprehension of basic general principles, by reference to which all particular apprehensions are tested and in virtue of which everything true wins approval but everything false is rejected. If any mistake could occur about these, then there could be no certainty in the entire subsequent apprehension.

Hence, in order that there can be some rightness in human deeds, there must be some enduring principle which has unchangeable rightness and by reference to which all deeds are tested, such that this enduring principle resists everything evil and gives assent to everything good. This is what *synderesis* is, whose job is to murmur back in reply to evil and to turn us towards what is good. Hence, it is to be admitted that it cannot do wrong.

Replies to arguments that synderesis *can do wrong*:

1 *Synderesis* is never cast down in its generalisations, but it can admit of error in the application of a general principle to something particular, as a result of incomplete or invalid deduction, or of some false assumption. Thus [the commentary] does not just say that *synderesis* is cast down, but that *conscientia*, which applies the general judgements of *synderesis* to particulars, is cast down.

2 When a false conclusion is drawn in some piece of reasoning from two propositions, of which one is true and the other false, the error in the conclusion is not attributable to the true one, but to the false one. Hence in that judgement by which the killers of the apostles thought that they did God a service, the sin did not come from the general judgement of *synderesis* that God's will is to be complied with, but from the false judgement of higher reason, which thought killing the apostles to be pleasing to God. Therefore it does not have to be allowed that they were disposed to sin by the actualisation of *synderesis*.

16.3 Is synderesis *extinguished in some people?*

Arguments that it is:

2 Unbelievers do not have any gnawing of *conscientia* about their lack of faith. But lack of faith is a sin. Hence, since it is the job of *synderesis* to murmur back against sin, it seems that it has been extinguished in them.

Discussion:

That *synderesis* is extinguished, can be understood in two senses. In one sense, with respect to the dispositional light itself: in this sense, it is just as impossible that *synderesis* should be extinguished as that the soul of a man should be deprived of the light of the active intellect, by which the primary premisses of theoretical and practical reasoning are made known to us. For this light belongs to the very nature of the soul, since it is in virtue of it that it is rational; it is said of this light 'The light of your face is sealed on us, Lord' (Psalm 4.6), i.e. so that it shows us what is good, for this was the reply to the question: 'Who will show us what is good?'

In the other sense, with respect to its actualisation, and this in two ways. In one, the actualisation of *synderesis* is said to be extinguished when its actualisation is totally obstructed. It occurs that the actualisation of *synderesis* is thus extinguished in those who have neither the use of free choice nor any use of reason; this can happen on account of an obstacle resulting from injury to organs of the body from which our reason needs to receive something. In the other way, because the actualisation of *synderesis* is turned aside to its contrary. It is impossible for *synderesis* to be extinguished thus in a general judgement, but in a particular judgement about what can be done it is extinguished whenever one sins in choosing. For the power of appetite or of something else to which one is subject so swallows up reason that, in choosing, *synderesis* does not apply the general judgement to the particular actualisation. But this does not extinguish *synderesis* without qualification, only relatively.

Replies to arguments that synderesis *is extinguished in some people:*

2 Among heretics, their *conscientia* does not murmur back against their lack of faith because of the error which is in their higher reason, as a result of which the judgement of *synderesis* is not applied to this particular [matter]. For the general judgement of *synderesis* remains in them, since they judge it evil not to believe what God has said, but they go astray in higher reason in this [particular], because they do not believe it to have been said by God.

17 Conscientia

17.1 Is conscientia a potentiality, a disposition or an actualisation?

Some people say that 'conscientia' can have three meanings. Sometimes 'conscientia' is used for the thing of which one is conscious, as 'belief' is used for the thing believed; sometimes for the potentiality by which we are conscious; sometimes for the disposition. Some people add that it is also sometimes used for the actualisation. The justification for these distinctions seems to be as follows. Because to be conscious of something is an actualisation, and one can consider, with respect to an actualisation, its object, potentiality, disposition and the actualisation itself, we sometimes find one noun which is used ambiguously for these four. E.g. the noun 'thought' sometimes signifies the thing thought (as names are said to signify thoughts), sometimes the thinking potentiality, sometimes a disposition, sometimes the actualisation. But in such classifications everyday usage should be followed, because words should be used as most people use them, as Aristotle says (Topics 2.2, 110a16). It seems, indeed, to be in accordance with everyday usage that 'conscientia' sometimes means the thing of which we are conscious, e.g. when someone says 'I'll tell you what's on my conscience', i.e. what is in my conscience. But this noun cannot be used, strictly speaking, for a potentiality or for a disposition, but only for an actualisation: this sense alone fits everything which is said about conscientia.

We should observe that it is unusual for a potentiality, actualisation and disposition to have the same name unless the actualisation is proper to the potentiality in question or the disposition in question, as seeing is proper to the visual potentiality, and knowing is actualisation to the disposition of knowledge: thus 'sight' sometimes names the potentiality, sometimes its actualisation, and 'knowledge' similarly. If, however, there is some actualisation which is suited to many or all dispositions or potentialities, it is unusual for any potentiality or any disposition to be named by such a word, as may be seen from the word 'use', which signifies the actualisation of any disposition and potentiality, since use is of that of which it is the actualisation. Hence the noun 'use' so signifies an actualisation that it can in no way signify a potentiality or disposition. And it seems to be the same with 'conscientia'. For the noun 'conscientia' signifies the application of knowledge to something, so that to be conscious of something (conscire) is, as it were, to know simultaneously (simul scire). But any knowledge can be applied to something, so '*conscientia*' cannot name some special disposition, or some potentiality, but names the actualisation which is the application of some disposition or other, or of something or other known, to a particular actualisation.

Something known, however, is applied to an actualisation in two ways; in the first, we consider whether there is or was an actualisation; in the second, we consider whether the actualisation is right or not. We are said to have consciousness of an actualisation in the first sense to the extent that we know whether that actualisation has occurred or not occurred, e.g. when, in everyday usage, it is said: 'I have no consciousness that this occurred', i.e. I do or did not know whether this has occurred or did occur. It is in this sense that Genesis 43:22, 'We have no consciousness of who put money in our sacks', and Koheleth 7:23, 'Your conscience knows that many times you have yourself cursed others', are to be understood. And it is in this sense that *conscientia* is said to bear witness to something, e.g. 'My conscience bears me witness' (Romans 9:1).

The second and other method of application by which something known is applied to an actualisation, in order to know whether the actualisation be right or not, takes two forms. In one, we are directed through the disposition of knowledge to do or not to do something. In the other, the actualisation is tested, after it has taken place, by the disposition of knowledge, for whether it be right or not right. These two forms of application correspond to two in theoretical matters, viz. to discovery and judgement. The form by which, through knowledge, we look at what should be done, as though taking advice, is comparable to discovery, by which we track down conclusions from premisses. But the form by which we test and discuss whether what has already occurred is right, is comparable to judgement, by which conclusions are traced back to premisses.

We use the word 'conscientia' in accordance with both types of application. When knowledge is applied to an actualisation in order to direct it, *conscientia* is said to goad or urge or bind us. But when knowledge is applied to an actualisation by way of testing what has already been done, *conscientia* is said to accuse or worry us if what has occurred is found to be out of accord with the knowledge by which it was tested, and to defend or excuse us if what has occurred is found to have turned out in accordance with the piece of knowledge.

But we should observe that in the first method of application, by which knowledge is applied to an actualisation to know whether it occurred, is an application to a particular actualisation of perceptory information, e.g. of memory (by which we recall what was done) or of perception, by which we perceive this particular actualisation which we now do. In the second and third types of application, however, in which we take counsel as to what should be done or test what is already done, dispositions of working reason are applied to the actualisation, viz. the disposition of *synderesis* and the disposition of wisdom, by which higher reason is perfected, and the disposition of knowledge, by which lower reason is perfected (whether all are applied simultaneously, or just one of them). For we test what we have done and take counsel as to what we should do by these dispositions. Testing, however, is not only of what has been done, but also of what should be done, whereas counsel concerns only what should be done.

17.2 Can conscientia be mistaken?

Arguments that it cannot:

7 A rule by which other things are governed must always be unfailingly correct. But *conscientia* is a rule of human deeds. Therefore *conscientia* must be correct.

Discussion:

I have argued that *conscientia* is no other than the application of knowledge to some special actualisation. Mistakes can occur in two ways in this application: first, because what is applied contains a mistake; second, because it is not applied properly. In the same way, mistakes in reasoning can occur in two ways: either because some false [premiss] is used, or because one does not reason correctly.

(1) That what is false is used, can happen on one side but cannot happen on the other. For it was argued above that the information [contained in] *synderesis* is applied by *conscientia*, and also higher and lower reason, to testing a particular actualisation. But since the actualisation is particular, while the judgement of *synderesis* is general, the judgement of *synderesis* cannot be applied to the actualisation without some particular premiss. It is sometimes higher reason and sometimes lower which provides this particularity, so that *conscientia* is completed by some reasoning about particulars, as it were. For example, if 'Nothing forbidden by the law of God ought to be done' is put forward by the judgement of *synderesis*, and 'Sexual intercourse with this woman is forbidden by the law of

God' is added from what is known to higher reason, then an application of *conscientia* is made in concluding: 'This sexual intercourse is to be refrained from.'

No mistake can occur in a general judgement of *synderesis*, as will be clear from what has been said above, but there can be sin in a judgement of higher reason, when someone thinks something to be in accordance with the [natural] law, or against it, which is not, e.g. heretics who believe that taking an oath has been forbidden by God. Here a mistake occurs in *conscientia* because of the falsity which was in the higher part of reason. Similarly, a mistake in *conscientia* can occur as a result of a mistake existing in the lower part of reason, e.g. when someone is mistaken about social norms of justice and injustice, what is honourable and what dishonourable.

(2) A mistake can also occur because the application in *conscientia* is not made in the right way, because, just as in reasoning about theoretical matters one can fail to use a valid form of argument and thereby the conclusion may be false, so, too, it can happen in the reasoning which is needed about what can be done, as has been said.

It is to be observed, however, that in certain cases *conscientia* can never make a mistake, viz. when there is a general judgement in *synderesis* about the particular actualisation to which *conscientia* is applied. For just as a mistake about particular conclusions which fall directly under general premisses expressed in the same terms cannot occur in theoretical reasoning, e.g. no one is deceived in making the judgement: 'This whole is greater than any of its parts', so, too, no *conscientia* can mistakenly judge: 'God is not to be loved by me' or 'Something bad ought to be done'. This is because in both kinds of judgement, the theoretical as much as the practical, the major premiss is known *per se*, as existing in a general judgement, and the minor premiss, too, by which the same thing is predicated of a particular instance of itself, e.g. 'Every whole is greater than any of its parts; but this is a particular whole; therefore, it is greater than any of its parts.'

Replies to arguments that conscientia *cannot be mistaken:*

7 *Conscientia* is not the first rule of human deeds but, rather, *synderesis*. *Conscientia*, however, is like a rule which is itself rule-governed (*regula regulata*), so there is nothing surprising if error can occur in it.

17.3 Does conscientia bind?

Without any doubt, *conscientia* binds. But, in order to see *how* it binds, we must observe that 'binding', used of spiritual things, is a metaphor taken from bodily ones, which implies the imposition of necessity. For someone who is bound is under the necessity of staying in the place where he is bound, and the power of moving somewhere else is taken away from him. So it is clear that binding has no place in what is necessary of itself, for we cannot say that fire is bound to be carried upwards, although it is necessary for it to be carried upwards. However, even in these cases of necessity, binding can have a place when the necessity is imposed by something else. There are two kinds of necessity which can be imposed by another agent. The first is a necessity of force, through which everything absolutely necessarily has to do what is determined by the action of the agent; the other should not strictly be called force but, rather, inducement. This is a conditional necessity, that is, deriving from a goal; e.g. there may be a necessity imposed upon someone that, if he does not do such-and-such, he will not obtain his reward.

The first kind of necessity, which is that of force, does not occur in changes of the will, but only in bodily things, because the will is naturally free from force. The second kind of necessity can be imposed upon the will, e.g. it may be necessary to choose such-and-such, if a certain good is to result, or if a certain evil is to be avoided. For, in such matters, to be without evil is tantamount to having what is good, as is clear from Aristotle (*Nicomachean Ethics* 5.1, 1129^{b}8). But just as the necessity of force is imposed on bodily things by some action, so conditional necessity is imposed upon the will by some action. The action by which the will is changed, however, is the command of a ruler or governor. Thus Aristotle says that a king is a source of change by his command (*Metaphysics* 5.1, 1013^{a}10). Thus the command of something which governs is related to binding bodily things by the necessity of force. But the action of a bodily agent only introduces necessity into another thing by its forceful contact with the thing on which it acts; so someone is only bound by the command of a ruler or lord, too, if the command reaches him who is commanded; and it reaches him through knowledge.

Hence no one is bound by an injunction except by means of knowledge of that injunction and, therefore, anyone who is not capable of being informed, is not bound by the command; nor is someone who is ignorant of an injunction of God bound to carry out the injunction, except in so far as he is obliged to know the injunction. But if he is neither obliged to know it nor does know it, he is in no way bound by the injunction. Just as in bodily matters a bodily agent only acts through contact, so in spiritual matters an injunction only binds through knowledge. And therefore, just as it is the same power by which touch acts and in virtue of which the agent acts, since touch only acts in virtue of the agent, and the power of the agent only by means of touch, so too, it is the same power by which an injunction binds and by which knowledge binds, since an injunction only binds in virtue of knowledge and knowledge only in virtue of the injunction. Hence, since *conscientia* is no other than the application of what is known to an actualisation, it has been shown that *conscientia* is said to bind by the power of divine injunction.

17.4 Does a mistaken conscientia bind?

There are various views on this. Some people say that *conscientia* can be mistaken both about things which are bad *per se* and about indifferent matters; a *conscientia*, therefore, which is mistaken about things which are bad *per se* does not bind but, about indifferent matters, does bind. But those who say this do not seem to understand what it is for *conscientia* to bind. For *conscientia* is said to bind because someone incurs sin unless he satisfies his *conscientia*, but not because someone who satisfies it does rightly. For otherwise advice would be said to oblige one, because in acting on advice, he does rightly. Yet we are said not to be bound by advice, because someone who ignores advice does not sin; whereas we are said to be bound by injunctions, because if we do not keep injunctions, we incur sin. *Conscientia* is not said to bind one to something, therefore, because if he does it for the sake of such a *conscientia*, it will be good, but because if he does not do it, sin will be incurred.

However, it does not seem possible for someone to escape sin if his *conscientia*, however much mistaken, tells him that something is an injunction of God which is indifferent or bad *per se* and, such *conscientia* remaining, he arranges to do the contrary. For so far as in him lies, by this itself he has the wish that the law of God be not observed; hence he sins mortally. So, although such a *conscientia*, which is mistaken, can be set aside, it is nevertheless obligatory so long as it remains, because he who transgresses it incurs sin of necessity. However, a correct and a mistaken *conscientia* bind in different ways; a correct *conscientia* binds without qualification and *per se*, but an erroneous *conscientia* relatively and accidentally.

I say that a correct *conscientia* binds without qualification, because it binds absolutely and in every circumstance. For if someone has a *conscientia* to avoid adultery, he cannot set aside this *conscientia* without sin, because, by mistakenly setting it aside, he would sin gravely, and while it remains, it cannot be by-passed in actualisation without sin. Hence it binds absolutely and in every circumstance. But a mistaken *conscientia* only binds relatively and conditionally. For someone whose *conscientia* tells him that he is obliged to fornicate, is not so obliged that he cannot forgo fornication without sin, except on condition that such a *conscientia* persists. But this *conscientia* can be removed without sin. Hence such a *conscientia* does not bind in every circumstance; something can happen, namely the laying aside of that *conscientia*, and, if this happens, then he is no longer bound. But what merely holds upon a condition is said to hold relatively.

I say that a correct *conscientia* binds *per se*, but an erroneous one accidentally. This will be clear from the following. Someone who wants or loves one thing on account of something else, loves that on account of which he loves the former *per se*, but loves accidentally, as it were, that which he loves on account of the other thing; e.g. a man who loves wine for its sweetness, loves sweetness *per se*, but the wine accidentally. A man who has a mistaken *conscientia* believing it to be correct (otherwise he would not be mistaken), however, does not cling to a mistaken *conscientia*, either, on account of the rightness which he believes to be there; he clings, rather – speaking *per se* – to a correct *conscientia*, but one which is mistaken as it were accidentally, to the extent that the *conscientia* which he believes to be right happens to be mistaken. Accordingly, speaking *per se*, he is bound by a correct *conscientia*, but speaking accidentally, by a mistaken one. This solution can be understood in the words of Aristotle, who asks practically the same question, viz. whether only a man who withdraws from correct reason is to be called intemperate, or also one who withdraws from false reason (*Nicomachean Ethics* 7.9, 1151ª29 ff). His solution is that the intemperate man withdraws from correct reason *per se*, but accidentally from false reason, and from the former without qualification, but from the latter relatively. What is *per se,* is without qualification, but what is accidental is relative.

Appendix 1

Medieval texts on conscience

This list is largely compiled from Lottin (1948), with additions at the beginning and end; it is almost certainly incomplete.

Peter Abelard (c. 1135), *Know Yourself*. Luscombe, D. E. (1971), Peter Abelard's *Ethics*. Oxford, at the Clarendon Press, pp. 53–77.

Udo (1173–1176), *Commentary on the 'Judgements' of Peter Lombard*. Lottin (1948), pp. 107–108.

Simon of Bisiniano (1173–1176), *Commentary on Gratian's 'Decretum'*. Lottin (1948), p. 74, n. 3.

Peter of Poitiers (1170s), *Commentary on the 'Judgements'* 2.14. Lottin (1948), pp. 108–109, n. 3.

Stephen Langton (1200–1206), *Questions*. Lottin (1957), pp. 59–61; (1948), pp. 112–115.

Godfrey of Poitiers (1213–1215). Lottin (1948), pp. 116–119.

Alexander Neckham (died 1217), *Speculum speculationum*. Lottin (1948), pp. 121–122.

William of Auxerre (1220–1225), *Summa aurea on the 'Judgements'*. Paris, Philippe Pigouchet, 1600. Excerpts from fol. 65va–fol. 66vb, in Lottin (1948), pp. 123–126, footnotes.

Hugo of St Cher (c. 1230), *Commentary on the 'Judgements'*. Lottin (1948), p. 127.

Roland of Cremona (c. 1230), *Questions on the 'Judgements'*. Lottin (1948), pp. 130–134.

William of Auvergne (1231–1236), *On the Soul* 7.13. In *Opera omnia* (ed. B. Le Feron), vol. 2, supplement, pp. 219–220. Paris, 1674, Re-print: Frankfurt, Minerva, 1963.

Philip the Chancellor. See Translations, pp. 94–109.

Anonymous (1). Lottin (1948), pp. 159–162.

Anonymous (2). Lottin (1948), pp. 164–167.

John of la Rochelle, *Summa de vitiis*. Lottin (1948), pp. 167–177, 359–364.

Anonymous (3). Lottin (1948), pp. 173–174.

Alexander of Hales (1220–1225), *Commentary on the 'Judgements'* 2.40. Lottin (1948), pp. 175–178.

[Alexander of Hales] (1240s), *Summa theologica* 2–1.4.1.2.3.4. Quaracchi, ex typographia Collegii S. Bonaventurae, 1928, vol. 2, pp. 491–500.

Alexander of Hales. Lottin (1948), pp. 356–357.

Anonymous Franciscan Masters. Lottin (1948), pp. 183–184, 185–186.

Anonymous (4). Lottin (1948), pp. 375–379.

Gauthier of Château-Thierry (died 1249), *Questions on Conscience*. Lottin (1948), pp. 188–196, 380–385.

Odo Rigaud (1241–1245), *Commentary on the 'Judgements'*. Lottin (1948), pp. 198–202.

Bonaventure. See Translations, pp. 110–121.

Albert the Great (c. 1242), *Summa de homine* 71. In *Opera omnia* (ed. A. Borgnet). Paris, Louis Vivès, 1890–1899, vol. 35, pp. 590 ff.

Albert the Great (c. 1248), *Questions on synderesis and on* conscientia. In *New Scholasticism* 9 (1935), pp. 312–322.

Aquinas (1253–1255), *Commentary on the 'Judgements'* 2.24.2.3–4.

Aquinas (1257–1258), *Debated Questions on Truth* 16–17. See Translations, pp. 122–136.

Aquinas (1266–1270), *Summa theologiae* 1.79.12, 13; 2–1.47.6; 2–1.94.1.

Peter of Tarento (1257–1259), *Commentary on the 'Judgements'* 2.39. Toulouse, Arnald Colomesius, 1649, vol. 2, pp. 327–331. Excerpts in Lottin (1948), pp. 237–238, footnotes.

Gauthier of Bruges (1267–1269), *Debated Questions* 12–16, 99. Ed. E. Longpré (1928). Louvain, *Les Philosophes belges*, vol. 10.

William de la Mare (c. 1274), *Commentary on the 'Judgements'*. Lottin (1948), pp. 242–245.

Henry of Ghent (1276), *Quodlibet* 1. Lottin (1948), pp. 246–247.

Richard of Mediavilla (1284–1287), *Commentary on the 'Judgements'* 2.39.2–3 (ed. F. Benzonus). Venice, L. Saardum, 1509.

Simon of Lens (1284–1287), *Commentary on the 'Judgements'* 2.39.1–4. Lottin (1948), pp. 251–253.

Peter John Olivi (1294–1296), *Questions on book 2 of the 'Judgements'* 81 (ed. B. Jansen). Quaracchi, ex typographia Collegii S. Bonaventurae, pp. 175–176.

Peter of Trabes (c. 1300), *Commentary on the 'Judgements'* 2.39.1–3. Lottin (1948), pp. 255–260.

Hannibald (1260–1262), *Commentary on the 'Judgements'* 2.39.4. In Aquinas, *Opera omnia*, Paris, Louis Vivès, 1871–1880, Vol. 30, pp. 427 ff.

Romano of Rome (1272–1273), *Commentary on the 'Judgements'*, 2.39.1–2. Lottin (1948), pp. 261–263.

John Quidort (1284–1286), *Commentary on the 'Judgements'*. Lottin (1948), pp. 264–267.

Humbert of Prully (1294), *Commentary on the 'Judgements'* 2.24.39. MS Bruges Ville 180, fol. 42^{va-vb}, fol. 51va.

Godfrey of Fontaines (1295), *Quodlibet* 12.2. (ed. J. Hoffman). Louvain, *Les Philosophes belges*, vol. 5, (1932), pp. 83–84.

Peter of Auvergne (1298), *Quodlibet* 2.16. Lottin (1948), pp. 269–270.

Bernard of Auvergne (c. 1300). Lottin (1948), pp. 272–273.

Anonymous (5). Lottin (1948), pp. 274–277, 279–283, 368–372.

Anonymous (6). Lottin (1948), pp. 285–291, 392–393.

Anonymous (7). Lottin (1948), pp. 293–297.

Anonymous (8). Lottin (1948), pp. 298–300.

Richard Fishacre (died 1248), *Commentary on the 'Judgements'* 2.24. Lottin (1948), pp. 302–303.

Richard of Cornwall (1250–1255), *Commentary on the 'Judgements'* 2.24. Lottin (1948), pp. 304–308.

Richard of Cornwall (1253–1255), *Summary of Bonaventure's Commentary on the 'Judgements'*. Lottin (1948), pp. 309–311.

Robert Kilwardby (1254–1261), *On Conscience*. Lottin (1948), pp. 313–316, 318–319, 321–325, 327–331.

Nicholas of Ockham (c. 1290), *Commentary on the 'Judgements'*. Lottin (1948), pp. 333–338.

John Duns Scotus (c. 1300), *Ordinatio* 2.39. *Opera omnia* (ed. L. Wadding), Lyons, 1639, vol. 13.

John Duns Scotus (1303), *Reportata Parisiensia* 2.39. *Opera omnia,* vol. 23, pp. 204 ff.

John Duns Scotus, *Quaestiones quodlibetales* 1.18. Paris, Johannes Parvus, 1513, fol. 18ᵃ.

Appendix 2

Programme for a medieval-philosophy course on conscience

1 POTENTIALITY AND ACTUALISATION (Background)

Texts:
Aristotle, *Metaphysics* 9; 5.12; *Physics* 8.4.

Readings:
C. D. Broad (1949), 'The "Nature" of a Continuant', in Feigl & Sellars (eds.), *Readings in Philosophical Analysis*, pp. 472–481. New York, Appleton-Century-Crofts.

A. J. P. Kenny (1964), translation of Aquinas, *Summa theologiae*, vol. 22, appendix 5. London, Blackfriars.

A. J. P. Kenny (1975), *Will, Freedom and Power*, chap. 7. Oxford, Basil Blackwell.

Questions:
What is the difference between potentiality and possibility?
Give your own examples to illustrate:
    (a) the difference between an active and a passive potentiality.
    (b) the difference between a rational and an irrational potentiality.
    Are Aristotle's criteria for these differences satisfactory?
What are the respective actualisations of *nous* (intellect, thought) and *orexis* (desire)?

2 DISPOSITIONS (Background)

Texts:
Aristotle, *Nicomachean Ethics* 1.13; 2.1–5; 6.1–4; *De anima* 3.6, 429^{b}3 ff; cf. also *Physics* 8.4, 255^{a}33 ff; *Metaphysics* 9.6, 1048^{a}34.

Readings:
G. Ryle (1949), *The Concept of Mind*, chap. 5. London, Hutchinson.

G. Ryle (1958), 'On Forgetting the Difference between Right and Wrong', in A. I. Melden (ed.), *Essays in Moral Philosophy*, pp. 147–159. Seattle, University of Washington Press. Re-printed in G. Ryle (1971), *Collected Papers*, vol. 2, pp. 381–390. London, Hutchinson.

P. T. Geach (1971), second edn., *Mental Acts*, chap. 3. London, Routledge and Kegan Paul.

G. H. von Wright (1963), *The Varieties of Goodness*, chap. 7. London, Routledge & Kegan Paul.

Questions:

How does Aristotle use his distinction between potentiality and actualisation to explain dispositions?

How are dispositions distinguished from other states?

To what extent are virtues like skills? Does Aristotle assimilate them too closely?

Explain the difference between theoretical (speculative) and practical *nous* (intellect), with examples. Is this the basis of Aristotle's distinction of virtue into intellectual and behavioural (moral)?

How is a mental disposition to be distinguished from a mental potentiality?

3 WEAKNESS OF WILL (Background)

Texts:

Plato, *Protagoras* 352–358; *Meno* 77c–89d; *Gorgias* 460a–b; *Republic* 4, 436a–441c.

Aristotle, *De anima* 3.9–11; *Nicomachean Ethics* 7.1–4.

Augustine, *Confessions* 7.3; 8.5–12; 10.30–41.

Readings:

R. M. Hare (1961), *The Language of Morals*, chaps. 10–11. Oxford, at the Clarendon Press.

R. M. Hare (1963), *Freedom and Reason*, chap. 5. Oxford, at the Clarendon Press.

A. J. P. Kenny (1963), *Action, Emotion and Will*, chap. 5. London, Routledge and Kegan Paul.

R. Robinson (1969), 'Aristotle on Akrasia', in *Essays in Greek Philosophy*, pp. 139–160. Oxford, at the Clarendon Press.

D. Davidson (1969), 'How is "Weakness of the Will" possible?', in J. Feinberg (ed.), *Moral Concepts*, pp. 93–113. London, Oxford University Press.

Questions:

What is the difficulty in supposing that a man can act voluntarily against his will?

Does weakness of will force us to distinguish, with Plato, between more than one subject of desires? or between different kinds of desire?

If contrary wishes are not logically inconsistent, why should they produce mental conflict?

Explain how Aristotle uses his distinction between potentiality and actualisation to offer a solution and assess the latter.

'The flesh lusteth against the spirit and the spirit against the flesh' (Galatians 5:17). Is this a paradigm for every conflict of wishes?

'I was bound not with the iron of another's chains, but by my own iron will . . '
Because my will was perverse it changed to lust, and lust yielded to become habit and habit not resisted became necessity. These were like links hanging one on another – which is why I have called it a chain – and their hard bondage held me bound hand and foot' (Augustine, *Confessions* 8.5). How far is what is done out of habit voluntary (N.B. 'done out of habit', not 'done habitually')? (Cf. Aquinas, *Summa theologiae* 2–1.78.2–3.)

'What I say I am doing and really desire to do for my health's sake, I do in fact for the sake of the enjoyment . . . often it is not at all clear whether it is the necessary care of my body calling for more nourishment, or the deceiving indulgence of greed wanting to be served. Because of this uncertainty my wretched soul is glad, and uses it as a cover and an excuse . . ., so that under the cloak of health it may shelter the business of pleasure' (Augustine, *Confessions* 10.31; cf. 10.33). 'For it is the most just punishment of sin, that each should lose what he would not use well; i.e. that he who knowing what is right does not do it, should lose the knowledge of what is right; and he who would not do well when he could, should lose the power when he would' (Augustine, *On Free Choice* 3. 18(52)). Is there a connection between weakness of will and self-deception?

Does weakness of will always involve conscience?

4 PRACTICAL REASONING (Background)

Texts:
Aristotle, *De motu animalium* 7; *Nicomachean Ethics* 6; 7.1–10.

Readings:
G. E. M. Anscombe (1957), *Intention*, §32–48. Oxford, Basil Blackwell.
M. Mothersill (1962), 'Anscombe's Account of the Practical Syllogism', in *The Philosophical Review* 70, pp. 448–461.
G. E. M. Anscombe (1963), 'Two Kinds of Error in Action', in the *Journal of Philosophy* 60, pp. 393–401.
R. M. Hare (1971), *Practical Inferences*. London, Macmillan.
J. K. K. Hintikka (1974), 'Practical *vs.* Theoretical Reason – An Ambiguous Legacy', in S. Körner (ed.), *Practical Reason*, pp. 83–102.
D. Locke (1974), 'Reasons, Wants and Causes', in the *American Philosophical Quarterly* 11, pp. 169–179.
A. J. P. Kenny (1975), *Will, Freedom and Power*, chaps. 5–6.
D. Wiggins (1976), 'Deliberation and Practical Reason', in *Proceedings of the Aristotelian Society* 76, pp. 29–51.

Questions:
In theoretical reasoning, validity preserves truth. What is the analogue of truth in practical reasoning?
Does practical reasoning normally conclude in an action, an intention, or what?
How are valid rules of practical reasoning related to valid rules of theoretical reasoning?
Is the deduction of deontic propositions theoretical or practical reasoning?

5 'SYNDERESIS'/'CONSCIENTIA'

Texts (from Translations):
Philip the Chancellor, 3; 2, appendix.
Bonaventure, 1.1; 2.1.
Aquinas, 16.2; 17.2.

Questions:
To what possible distinction between two senses in which *we* speak of 'conscience'
does the medieval distinction point?
How far was it satisfactorily drawn by medieval writers?

6 CONSCIENCE AND REASON

Texts (from Translations):
Augustine, *On the Trinity* 12.
Philip the Chancellor, 2.
Bonaventure, 1.2.
Aquinas, 16.1; 17.1.

Questions:
Is conscience related to belief or to knowledge?
Are any of its dictates apprehended intuitively? Are any of them *a priori?*
What are the difficulties in identifying conscience with reason?
If it is a disposition, how does it differ from belief or from knowledge?

7 THE MEANING OF 'OUGHT'

Texts (from Translations):
Bonaventure, 1.2.
Aquinas, 17.3.

Readings:
I. Kant (1786, second edition), *Groundwork of the Metaphysic of Morals.* Translated
    by H. J. Paton (1948) under the title *The Moral Law,* pp. 402–404, 413–421
    (pages of the German edition, printed by Paton in the margin). London,
    Hutchinson.
R. M. Hare (1952), *The Language of Morals,* part I.

Questions:
Is the meaning of 'ought' to be explained by appeal to a logical mood (e.g. imper-
ative, optative)?
Do deontic sentences have truth-values?
Are deontic sentences disguised hypotheticals? If so, what are their antecedents?
If not, how (if at all) is the meaning of 'ought' in moral contexts related to its
meaning in non-moral contexts?
Can grounds be adduced for accepting moral principles, or only causes?

8 CONSCIENCE AND EMOTION

Texts (from Translations):
Philip the Chancellor, 4.
Bonaventure, 2.1, 2.
Aquinas, 16. 1 *ad* 7; 16.2, 3; 17.3.

Readings:
J. Butler (1726), *Fifteen Sermons,* nos. 7, 10, in W. E. Gladstone, *The Works of
Joseph Butler, D. C. L.* Oxford, at the Clarendon Press, 1897.

D. Stafford-Clark (1952), *Psychiatry Today*, pp. 116–119. London, Penguin Books.
R. E. D. Markillie, 'Conscience and Guilt', forthcoming in a volume ed. M. Jeeves, London, Inter-Varsity Press.

Questions:
Is there any difference between guilt and remorse? Are they emotions and, if so, how related to other emotions?
Is either of them conceptually related to conscience? Does the answer have any bearing upon the issue whether conscience is innate or acquired?
Is it conceivable that a person should lack a conscience altogether (e.g. through having been born without one, having failed to acquire one, or subsequently having lost it)?

9 MISTAKEN CONSCIENCE

Texts (from Translations):
Philip the Chancellor, 3.
Bonaventure, 2.3.
Aquinas, 17.2, 4.

Questions:
'It no more follows that, if a person believes that he ought to ϕ, then he ought to ϕ, than it follows that, if a person believes that p, then p. So we are not bound by our consciences.' Do you agree?
Are there any circumstances in which it is not an acceptable excuse for a person to plead that he acted in accordance with his conscience?

10 CONSCIENCE AND PSYCHOLOGICAL CLASSIFICATIONS

Texts (from Translations):
Jerome.
Philip the Chancellor, 1.
Bonaventure, 1.1; 2.1.
Aquinas, 16.1; 17.1.

Questions:
Can mental activity be distinguished into theoretical and practical in a way which will accommodate conscience?
Is there a psychological potentiality to which conscience can be assigned? If so, is conscience a disposition or an actualisation of that potentiality, or are these categories inadequate to describe it accurately?

Bibliography

Davies, W. D. (1970). *Paul and Rabbinic Judaism*. London, S.P.C.K.

Davies, W. D. (1962). 'Conscience', in Buttrick *et al.* (eds.), *The Interpreter's Dictionary of the Bible*. Nashville, N.Y., Abingdon Press. Vol. 1, pp. 671–676.

Hintikka, J. K. K. (1957). 'Necessity, Universality and Time in Aristotle', in *Ajatus*. Vol. 20, pp. 65–90.

Hintikka, J. K. K. (1962). *Knowledge and Belief: an introduction to the logic of the two notions*. Ithaca, Cornell University Press.

Kenny, A. J. P. (1975). *Will, Freedom and Power*. Oxford, Blackwell.

Lewis, C. S. (1967). *Studies in Words*. Cambridge, Cambridge University Press. Chap. 8: 'Conscience and Conscious', 181–213.

Lottin, O. (1957, 1948). *Psychologie et morale aux XIIe et XIIIe siècles*, vol. 1 (second edition), vol. 2. Gembloux, J. Duculot.

Moore, G. F. (1927). *Judaism in the First Centuries of the Christian Era*. Cambridge, Harvard University Press.

Newman, J. H. (1849). *Discourses Addressed to Mixed Congregations*. London, Longman, Brown, Green and Longmans, No. 5: 'Saintliness the Standard of Christian Principle'.

Pierce, C.A. (1953). *Conscience in the New Testament*. London, S. C. M. Press. Studies in Biblical Theology. No. 15.

Potts, T. C. (1971). 'Aquinas on Belief and Faith', in J. Ross (ed.), *Inquiries into Medieval Philosophy*. Westport, The Greenwood Publishing Company. Pp. 3–22.

Potts, T. C. (1976). 'Philosophy as Pure Linguistics', in C. Perelman (ed.) *Philosophie et langage*. Institut des hautes études de Belgique.

Ryle, G. (1958). 'On Forgetting the Difference between Right and Wrong', in A. I. Melden (ed.), *Essays in Moral Philosophy*. Seattle, University of Washington Press. Re-printed in G. Ryle (1971), *Collected Papers*. London, Hutchinson. Vol. 2, pp. 381–390.

Strack, H. L., and Billerbeck, P. (1928). *Kommentar zum Neuen Testament aus Talmud und Midrasch*. Band 4. Munich, Beck.

Wittgenstein, L. (1953). *Philosophical Investigations*. Oxford, Blackwell.

Wittgenstein, L. (1967). *Zettel*. Oxford, Blackwell.

Wittgenstein, L. (1969). *On Certainty*. Oxford, Blackwell.

Analytical index of subjects

(excluding Appendix 2)

Much of the material to be indexed under 'synderesis' and 'conscientia' lends itself better to a matrix than to lists; accordingly, a matrix for each of these terms is placed first. Further entries under each term are to be found in the subsequent list of subjects.

Index of proper names

Does not include Appendices or Bibliography.
Translations and discussions of them indicated by bold type.

Index of Biblical references